TROUT WATER

TROUT
WATER

A Year on the Au Sable

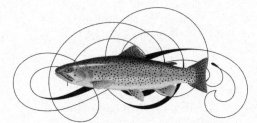

JOSH GREENBERG

MELVILLE HOUSE
BROOKLYN • LONDON

TROUT WATER

First published in March 2021 by Melville House

Copyright © Josh Greenberg, 2021
All rights reserved

First Melville House Printing: January 2021

Melville House Publishing
46 John Street
Brooklyn, NY 11201

and

Melville House UK
Suite 2000
16/18 Woodford Road
London E7 0HA

mhpbooks.com
@melvillehouse

ISBN: 978-1-61219-901-6
ISBN: 978-1-61219-902-3 (eBook)

Library of Congress Control Number 2020950777

Designed by Euan Monaghan
Printed in the United States of America

1 3 5 7 9 10 8 6 4 2

A catalog record for this book is available
from the Library of Congress

TABLE OF CONTENTS

TROUT WATER

INTRODUCTION

I originally meant this book to imitate one of my very favorite pieces of fly-fishing literature, John Waller Hills's *A Summer on the Test*, but like with most things I begin (be it chicken coop or fishing outing) the end result differs greatly from my vision at the start. Some of this is material: my summer on the Au Sable, like all summers on the Au Sable, was different from the year before, and *much* different from the year it is now, 2020. Some of this is simply accounted for by my own nature, my propensity to constantly revisit, self-edit, question, and, finally, push forward on what seems at the time to be the best path. In this way, in my life, I often feel like I'm walking through a thick Michigan bog, just trying to find the river.

This is my second attempt at an outdoor journal. The first, in New Zealand, fizzled into its clear rivers. But, while incomplete, and at times laughably bad, that first attempt provided the basis for this book. I recorded my entries at night as my kids settled into sleep in the bedroom next to my fly-tying room. The lateness of such entries undoubtedly colored my perception, just like every minute of every day colors our perceptions.

But the Au Sable being a night river, and I being a night owl, it seems appropriate for the words to be hatched under starlight.

Because I don't cover it in the text, a simple introduction: I grew up in Ohio but spent my summers working at Gates Au Sable Lodge in Grayling, Michigan. Over time I've tied flies, served food, made beds, guided anglers, loaded reels, and, a little later in life, understood contracts, taxes, and balloon payments. But it's the river outside the lodge, and the people that it connects, that has bound me to the business. And it's the loss of these river people that is really the most difficult part of this job. Thinking for the dead is foolish, I know, but it helps. So in this way, this book is for those I've met and lost along the banks of the Au Sable, and whom I visit often for what I think of as their advice.

As this pandemic swept through our real and virtual lives, the river has served as a sanctuary for people on both sides of a supposedly divided country. Owning a fly-fishing lodge on a popular river in a state split almost down the middle right and left allows me a top-view of a clientele equally similar and different, though it seems, powered by social media, that these differences are just more fun to defend ad infinitum, a doubling down on convictions that tend, in my opinion, to stray further and further from reality. If one fly-fished in such a manner, not a trout would be caught. Because trout *are* caught, I keep the faith that the greatest lessons of trout water haven't been lost on us.

Josh Greenberg

CHAPTER 1: TERRY IN THE BARDO

Every man takes the limits of his own field
of vision for the limits of the world.

—ARTHUR SCHOPENHAUER, Studies in Pessimism

May 5

When you're waiting on the phone call that will inform you a friend has died, the only place I know to go is the river. It was evening when I arrived, and that's when you look for rising trout on the Au Sable in May: when the river is silver with sky reflection and the edges are dark beneath the cedars.

It was almost too early in the year to be looking for evening spinners, but I wasn't looking for evening spinners. I was looking for the river. Only after I'd found the river, and sat on the bank edge, did I look for evening spinners. And, surprisingly, there they were: a small flight of Hendrickson spinners. They trailed unnaturally bright, seemingly luminescent yellow egg sacs—the only spot of color in this repressed spring.

Okay, I thought. So maybe there'll be some fishing to go

with the phone call. Even to just see a trout rise would mean spring. I had a box of Hendrickson spinners I'd tied over the winter. There's not much I like better than trying out a bunch of winter-tied flies on the first rising trout of the spring. There were no trout rising yet, and there wouldn't be many in the high water. Many of the trout would be full with washed-in earthworms. The cold water would make them sluggish. But just one evening rise can alter the worldview of a spring-starved angler.

I stood and began to hunt slowly upstream, walking the bank. The river was high and fast, but smooth. The Au Sable is the perfect canvas on which to paint a rise. I saw no rises, however. I saw hardly any life in any form. There was no one in the valley. No one. The river cabins stood empty, their owners downstate or somewhere south, and the cabins had broken branches on their roofs and in their yards, detritus from the long winter. There were no cars or barking dogs or canoers. The river was one cloudburst from being blown out. It was still so brown and quiet, the trees still barren; you'd have thought it was a warmish November evening.

I was determined to find a rising fish. No blind-fishing of any sort: rising trout or bust. I snuck through the flooded shore grass and alders, hunting the surface for rings. Further up the flooded bank, I had to pick through some beaver work. I'd trapped a beaver from this same bank this past winter and used the fur to tie the body of the fly on my hook keeper. I try to examine life, but not fishing and hunting, which I love. It is not an addiction. The examined life is preferred, but it's dangerous to examine love.

⌁

Tiger Woods said once that he could will in a putt. In his prime, I think he could. Sometimes I think I can will a rise. I can't. But when it happens, it *feels* like *I* made it happen, even though I've unsuccessfully attempted to will tens of thousands of others.

This evening, I *willed* a trout to rise. It was just above the upstream corner of a submerged dock, at the tail of a seam that has always been a solid-gold, early-season dry fly spot. The rise was purposeful—and though I watched it happen, it seemed I'd somehow caught the tail end of it. I thought of all those astro-types scanning the cosmos for the afterimages of enormous events. A star exploded ten million years ago and they just now saw it. That's like the rings of an early spring rise, if you ask me. A silver dollar-sized bubble spun in the eddy by the dock . . . the last known proof of what, to me, seemed a cosmic happening. My eardrums picked up my heartbeat as if I needed proof of my excitement. The trout fed again. Carelessly? Maybe. But it had pushed toward the bank, away from the seam, closer to the small backwater spinning above the dock. Maybe even in the backwater. That rise was followed by one back in the seam and three feet upriver, nearer the original rise. It threw a beautiful curved bow wave. Left a nice bubble.

I decided to fish from my knees, perhaps unnecessarily, as the trout was forty feet away and unlikely to spook from my standing there. The Hendrickson spinners humped along their eggs for upstream deposit, but there weren't too many bugs and I didn't think there could be many on the water. This evening-rising trout was a rare find indeed; the sort of fleeting treasure—rainbow, meteor—that can be possessed without actually being captured by hook or camera. It belonged to no one, but it was all mine.

❧

When I first met Terry Warrington he, like me, was working at the fly shop. It was my first job ever, and would be his last job ever. He'd just finished being a fly fisher of the world. Atlantic salmon may be the aristocratic fish, but not all Atlantic salmon anglers are aristocrats. Terry pursued Atlantic salmon in the famous, faraway places before settling, in retirement from academia, on the Au Sable. He was a science-driven guy, effusive, affable, odd. He wore enormous fit-over sunglasses. Once, at his house, I saw that he had a half-dozen identical fit-over sunglasses on a shelf near the front door.

He and his wife kept a large garden at their house. Both were retired chemistry educators. Terry could talk and talk— and talk. His stories were a series of footnotes that wandered across time and space. For example, we were once talking about tying flies using deer hair for the bodies, and he was suddenly talking about why he quit deer hunting, which was because he had gotten into a gunfight with another deer hunter. He didn't think of it as a gunfight. But some guy fired near him, so Terry fired back, and this escalated into a volley of gunfire, and that, I told Terry, is how I define a gunfight. At such times he'd pause, and then say, "What were we talking about again?" And, should you remember the starting point, a different set of footnotes would begin, headed off in a different, usually trout-y, direction.

When he was old and locally famous, many knew Terry from his time on the bench at Gates Lodge, the fishing resort on the Au Sable where we both worked. He could hardly wade by then, so he fished off the bench almost every morning and evening that the trout might rise. But when I met Terry in the late 1990s, he—while no longer a fly fisher of the world— fished *all* of the Au Sable, and *all* of the Manistee, and chased steelhead on the Pere Marquette River and went on adventures with his pal Mike Bachelder on the Rifle River, or for smallmouth on the lower Au Sable.

These were the halcyon days. I had a crew I fished with (and still do, mostly the same crew) and Terry, forty years our senior, was part of it. He'd night fish down through the Sucker Hole, and then be up early to look for dimpling trout in the currents of his beloved Whirlpool. I did not see him age, but then again, I saw him every day. I did not understand when lodge guests, separated from us for half a year, noticed—before we did—that Terry wasn't chasing hex on the Manistee, or night fishing the South Branch, and was spending more and more time on the bench at the dock on the lodge.

Some of this was a legitimate and natural change of taste and pace. He preferred dry flies. Then, he preferred dry flies cast at rising fish. Then, a few health scares. He did not wade by himself. He rarely fished the South Branch. His beloved North, and the late-fall, blue-winged olive mayflies, became too cold. More and more often, he fished at the bench at the lodge. It was, for years, the launching pad to short forays— no more than fifty-yard wades—to the Fence Run, the Bread Hole, the new run on the far side of the island, or the flat by Rusty's Pew (a bench installed by the river at the lodge). As a gardener of small spaces, he treaded lightly lest he spook the run and ruin his night. An angler truly understands what Robert Traver meant by "hoarding the cast," when he has only the stamina to fish a single small run in an evening . . . and must fish knowing one bad cast would be his last of the night. These runs were everything to Terry. They encapsulated in miniature everything he loved grandly. In the summer, when the small flies were around, Terry was always on the bench. Always. He became his own little run, a place that the rest of us could visit for compassion, advice, understanding, humor, memories, gossip, chemistry, gardening. In this way, he became to us anglers somewhat indistinguishable from the river.

From his pulpit he amused us shopworkers, yelling "Drag!" and "Wrong!" to other fly fishers who were unprepared to face the criticism of both the trout and the dude on the bench. But, if they were willing, Terry would take these same folks and show them his fifteen-foot leaders and boxes of CDC blue-winged olives, and give them hope (and a leader and some flies) and teach them what it meant to get a drag-free drift, and to match the hatch, and in that way the lives of many were redirected toward the path of the angle.

Ultimately, the river was too fast, and he was confined to the bench run: a small gravel flat punctuated by swaying weeds and a few sand swales that twisted the current into what Terry found to be a satisfying and unsolvable puzzle, and within these twists of current were the ten or twelve trout that, last summer and fall, would be the final trout he'd cast at. One day he'd take a seemingly small stumble in his home . . . and it would start a bleed within him. This was how it began, and what would lead to the end.

Working a fly shop presents many challenges, the greatest being that you will watch people fade, one spring to the next, until your phone rings. What would it be like when Terry was officially gone? Because though he was gone, he was not gone yet. He was somewhere between. He was going, going . . . Earlier that week, I'd gone to the bench for solace from the sadness of losing a person who had become a fixture in my existence. But, in arriving at the bench, I realized no solace, since the giver of the solace was also, through his absence, the giver of my grief. Losing loved ones hurts twice that way.

I knew he'd become, once dead, someone I'd reimagine in my mind, as if to keep him alive. It could be as simple as a fly change: What would Terry use on this fish by the dock? Probably his CDC Hendrickson spinner. What would the legendary Rusty Gates use? Probably the spinner with the wings made of rabbit foot, would be my guess. They'd disagree on flies, maybe even argue about it. But then, later, they'd agree on the importance of making that first cast count and getting a drag-free drift. They'd tell me there is a difference between the act of living and the act of dying. I saw them do both, and I think they'd agree on that.

∽

It wasn't a difficult cast to reach the dock fish, and I'd made the very same cast before over the years, because it's a good dock in a good stretch of river. Probably, I figured, I'd thrown casts at this very same fish the year before. Maybe I'd even caught it. I'd had a great night in this run in 2018. None of this quelled my nerves. Normally I savor such excitement. But these felt like the anticipatory tremors of a cosmic fuckup. When I pulled line from the reel, the drag mechanism seemed so loud that I quit pulling for a second, fearing it would spook the trout.

Stupid, stupid, I whispered.

I false-casted a few times to measure distance and to shake off six months of weighted lines and weighted flies. By the time I laid the line down it seemed this cast and this fish were the most important event in several millennia. The fly dropped way too far past the seam and held up in the very top of the backwater. I lifted the rod to skitter the fly into position and lowered the rod tip and fed line into the drift. Three feet, two feet, one foot. Keep feeding this line, I thought, the fish could be following it down.

The fly floated toward the dock. It bobbed along the dock. It swept past the dock. I kept feeding line into the drift. Breathe. Breathe. Dammit. Damn fish. I slowly recovered the line. I remained kneeling on that sloppy bank, watching the dock, unmoving, for fifteen rise-less minutes. The Hendricksons were gone from the air. The river was lifeless and dead. A female mallard swam between the flooded alders behind me. She swam within feet of me. I exchanged a few quiet words with her. I told her it looked like a one-cast night. She swam past, weaving out of the alders and crossing the main river. I looked back to the dock. Tried to will it. The sky had transformed from sunset to cyan.

I could wait on the dock fish to rise again, or try to find another. Easy choice.

I walked downstream—far downstream—up to (and maybe just past) a NO TRESPASSING sign, so I could stand across from an artesian well and check the bubble line. Nothing. *But somewhere*, I thought, *somewhere there is a trout rising.* I returned, at a jog, to the dock and stood where I'd kneeled earlier. Impatient, I left, and then bushwhacked upstream because the angler trail was underwater. I climbed a small bluff that allowed a long look upstream. The river was polished silver. The evening was just about finished. *But somewhere . . .*

I ran—*ran*—back downstream to the artesian well, jingling and clanking. A running angler sounds like a cardboard box of dishware falling down a stairway, especially in the quiet of a late spring. Threading through the flooded alders, I slowed, finally, and came to what would have been the edge of the river if the river weren't swollen. The bubble line was visible, but the far side of the river had merged with the shadows. In a month, this would be prime time. In a month and a half, I'd be here too early in the evening, and there'd be other anglers here, stationed every fifty feet, waiting for the main-event bugs of June. The river would be alive, the bank grasses green and thick, the fireflies bleating lights. My own kids, like this year's spring, had arrived well past the due date. The hand-wringing of waiting, the imagining of the future, the unexpected vibrancy of arrival, I couldn't live properly without the seasons of temperate places.

I thought to myself, *hold*. Just hold here. No use running back to the dock. No use trying to keep alive what is already lost. The event was nearly done, with just one rising trout and one unsuccessful cast. My boots were up to the ankles in muck. The phone would ring within the next day. Though Terry was already gone, he wasn't gone already. He was somewhere in-between. The fly fisher knows this space between day and night, and hunts the bardo for rises.

That trout I caught that night . . . it was rising in the bardo. And it wasn't more than fifteen feet from me, in flat water the color of slate, in dead crap water, in the barren muck-bottomed pig wallow that barely passes for chub habitat, she rose far inside of the bubble line and the trickling artesian well across the river. It was a controlled plop. I froze. Another plop, three feet upstream of the previous. The tip of its tail signed the surface: *one good trout, rising here.*

I flipped the fly in front of the rise.

Please. This was no longer an act of will. This was pleading. It had been a long cold spring. Wouldn't it be something if this unexpected trout would just . . . ? The concentration that eludes me when I'm filling out tax forms or reading the fine print of an insurance policy is found when it is directed at a dry fly floating toward a rising trout. I could see the individual hackles of the fly, the press of the knot into the syrupy meniscus. Then, I could see something immediately behind the fly, appearing within the water, coalescing. *Is that . . . ?*

It was! It was the face of a brown trout that loomed through the watery gloaming, my fly floating right between its eyes.

Holy shit!

I was once looking out my kitchen window, into a dark night, when my youngest son's face appeared beyond the reflection, cloaked in a white hockey mask. He'd gone outside and had been standing there, he said, for some time. All these other dimensions are around us, concealed merely by reflection. I'd leapt from my chair. He came running inside laughing. The effect of this trout was similar, but I clenched instead of spooking. My breath was shaped silently into curses. The surroundings of the night vanished into a pithy point of electricity that comes with four eyes being trained, simultaneously, on a size 14 fly.

I thought it would eat the fly several times. But no, this fish was willing to hover a centimeter below the surface and follow my imitation downstream, the rest of its body materializing behind the face. It was as close as a trout could be to a fly without eating it. It followed it downstream two feet. Six feet. Ten feet. I swear. That trout glowed gold-silver in the half-dark. It was like looking for Orion and seeing the god-warrior in splendid whole, instead of just a few bright stars.

When the trout ate, it did so without forward movement or attack. It was so close to the fly it simply opened its mouth and let the fly and surrounding water fall in. The water was strained through the gills. The fly was impaled in the corner of its mouth. It leapt wildly three times, each successive leap wilder than the previous. It pulled drag out toward the bubble line, tired, and fought in a series of shortening rushes before I landed it on the flooded bank and held it. A brown trout as pewter as the river, a dark-nickel female with an even mix of ebony and red spots . . . though the red was more mahogany. If an artist were to form a trout from the water it lived in, this would be the finished product.

I released it, and the last sign of life left with it. When I stood, the river was dead. The woods were sullen. Not even a spring peeper. I checked my phone but there were no texts or missed calls. Instead of being elated, I was spooked. I hustled through the woods to my vehicle and left in my waders, something I never do. I drove behind the eyes of the headlights with a trickle of chill along my skin. The phone didn't ring. Just bleated a text. I think. I don't remember how or when, exactly. At one point the phone call was very important to me. But once it happened, I didn't think much of it. I just remember the next day the bench was empty and the Hendricksons were hatching and the trout were rising. That's what I remember.

CHAPTER 2: THE SKIN-WALKER

But Mouse, you are not alone,
In proving foresight may be vain:
The best laid schemes of mice and men
Go often askew

—ROBERT BURNS, "To a Mouse, on Turning Her Up
in Her Nest with the Plough, November, 1785"

May 30

The other day I was thinking about old Tom the fly tyer, and
how a conversation from years ago led me to meet—and flee—
my skin-walker.

Old Tom was a commercial fly tyer, and, until he got too
old, he could spin some pretty nice flies. Tom was mostly deaf,
and could have used an ear trumpet to supplement his hearing
aids. He was a yeller and you had to be a yeller too. We'd stand
in the fly shop and yell at each other. Finally, with enough
yelling and diagrams, an agreement was reached on what the
fly should look like, and how many he should tie. I remember

once he looked at Rusty's sample and yelled, "I'll tie them for you but they won't look like that!"

Tom was also an excellent fly caster and so, when we found him standing in the river in his hip boots, us guides would have to wait for him to lay down a cast and then push the boat as fast as we could to get out of the way of his back cast, because he wouldn't be able to hear us even if we yelled. Most of the time, I don't think he even noticed a boat had gone behind him.

Anyway, one day he was in the shop describing how shitty the trout fishing on the Au Sable had become. To him, the fishery had really gone downhill.

He shook his head.

He stared at me and frowned.

"It used to be you'd hear all sorts of big fish rising at night! Now when I go out at night I don't hear a darn thing!"

Because of this memory of old Tom the fly tyer, I met my skin-walker.

⁓

That talk with Tom was years ago, but the memory of him lamenting the fishing on the Au Sable bubbled back to the surface this cold, high-water spring. The fishing on the mainstream had been poor, and so the attitude around the fly shop was also poor. Andy Grant, a young fly fisher who works at the fly shop, looked at me and said in his deliberate way: "When I can't catch a fish, I usually blame myself. But on the Au Sable, everyone seems to blame the river." I'd heard bad reports for the last two weeks from the Holy Waters—a famous stretch of the mainstream—even as the rest of the river system began to fish more or less like it should. It seemed a good excuse to go fish "the Holies," as we call it, and see if I thought it was a problem of the river or a problem of the angler. This is not to assert that I would fare differently, but there's a difference between a river fishing poorly and a poor fishery. A poor fishery doesn't have enough fish to catch. A river fishing poorly has plenty of fish, but for whatever reason—weather, angler ineptitude—the trout prove elusive. What better place to conduct my "study" than in old Tom's home water? The last place he liked to fish was just upstream of the lodge, where a long flat fell into a half-mile of riffles.

The evening was cold, gray, windy, and just warm enough. *Just warm enough*, in May, is anything over sixty degrees.

It's a beautiful stretch of river. Working upstream, it begins in a wide, shallow riffle that is increasingly pinched by a series of cedar sweeps, resulting in a rollicking surface with enough shade, cover, and cobbles to create the sort of pocket water that is rarely found on the Au Sable. This is perfect water for blind-fishing—that is, casting toward likely looking spots instead of at rising trout. The blind-fishing angler uses the dry fly like a mining pick. I hoped to find a good fish willing to surreptitiously rise for a dry fly in the chop.

The chute at the head of this riffle is difficult to wade through. Upstream of the chute are several hundred yards of flat evening water. Such divisions are almost always the best trout water.

I worked up the riffle casting a #18 CDC caddis into the wind, which, like any fly-fishing done into the wind, wasn't particularly pleasant. The river was still too fast to wade up the middle so I stayed on the south bank, standing behind logjams and fishing the water in front of them. The river was coffee-colored; it was April water in mid-May, as foreboding as it had been the evening Terry had died. Spring just wouldn't spring. The water felt cold and wrong, somehow seemed tinged with snow. I caught a couple of the small brook trout that were leaping in the backwaters toward some caddis. So much for my big surreptitious riser. For May, or any of the spring and summer months, this was slow fishing. The problem, I figured, wasn't the trout population, but the above-average and dingy water flow. At its best, the Au Sable is a clear river with magic in its shadows and mayfly spinners dancing over the riffles. This was not its best.

I exited halfway up the riffle, bummed, and walked the trail up to the flat water. The flat water is dotted with human-made structures, some of them dating back to the Civilian Conservation Corps days, when hundreds of young men were stationed on the Au Sable and, among other things, were charged with making trout habitat structures—wooden raft-type things that sit in the river and shelter trout from predators. It's a great stretch of water and I always think of those CCC boys toiling around in that river. The river looked a lot different back then. The surrounding land had been mowed flat from the logging days and the river flowed through an unlikely prairie, baking in the sun, until humans placed enough of the trout habitat structures—and stocked enough trout—for the river to eventually grow into a wild trout fishery. And every few years, humans have to put habitat in again.

The flat-water section is tough to blind-fish. It has little in the way of seams or bubble lines to really concentrate the trout. To blind-fish it properly you'd have to move very slowly and cover all the water and this, while pleasurable to some, is not pleasurable to me. Instead, I paced the bank anxiously, waiting for the trout to rise. In hunting, this is known as spot and stalk. There were a few spinners gathering, pushed to mate earlier by the cold air. Some caddis fluttered by the bankside alders. The river was quiet.

I walked the trail up to the start of a second set of riffles without seeing a single rise.

"It's a bit dead," I said to myself. "It's really a bit dead."

There was another angler up in the second set of riffles, a portly late-middle-aged fellow. He was sitting on the bank, butt on a hummock of grass, boots in the water. He was a real throwback, fedora, stogie, faded vest, and lots of knickknacks. He was tying on a fly, and at arm's length, and I wondered if he'd lost his glasses.

It wasn't an easy spot to get to. He must have arrived at the parking spot after me and then walked up along the secret trail on the north bank while I fished the chute. Somehow he'd walked past me unheard, despite all the jangles on his vest. I stayed crouched in the forest and spied on him for a bit. He stood up from the bank, checked behind him, and threw a quick reach cast toward the middle of the river. He fed some line into the drift. Then he collected his line, sat down on the bank, and began the process of selecting another fly, holding his boxes as far from his eyes as he could.

"That son of a bitch must have a riser," I whispered. I say these things all the time. I don't mean anything by it.

I snuck off, walking downstream. I decided to wait on a nice little seam between two leaning cedars, one of the few river features in that stretch, and a place, over the years, where the trout have risen even on barren nights. And as I snuck along the trail, moving more slowly now, I saw a disturbance in the seam, and another, and knew there were trout rising.

Three trout, in fact, were rising consistently. Around them, up and down the flat water, other nice trout began rising sporadically. Some of these sporadic risers were nice fish . . . nicer than the three consistent trout. I tried to sneak in on some of them, but they weren't rising but once every ten minutes, if that, and weren't worth the trouble. I figured with all the high cold water the trout were full on worms and other things, and their metabolism had slowed to the point that aggressive feeding was unnecessary. There were some spinners on the water, even a few Hendricksons still, as well as the *Leptophlebia*, which we call brown bugs, sulphur spinners (the 16s, which are alternatively known as yellow-wing sulphurs and light Hendricksons), and, yes, I could see them now, a persistent little hatch of sulphur duns. This would be a good night. There were trout in this river. It was just a terrible spring. It had been a spring of high water and loss.

I was trying to sneak in on those big, inconsistent fish, and it wasn't working. I had a little conversation with myself that went something like: *You're going to get skunked if you keep pursuing the trout you can't catch.* I went to work on the three trout that were consistently rising. They were all in good places. The top fish was rising in the two-inch eddy behind a stick. The middle fish was moving in and out of a bubble line. The bottom fish was skating a slick little tail-out. All three rose for, and then refused, my fly—a generic spinner imitation we refer to as a "Brown Bug"—on fine tippet. I tied on a long section of even finer tippet and the sulphur mayfly imitation and rose all three trout and landed two, a ten-inch brook trout and a thirteen-inch brown trout. Not bad. Aside from a few small ones from the margins it was a mediocre but passable evening for a tough spring. The trout weren't all dead. The river was still cold and high with run-off and rain. I remembered a couple of old clients who used to come up to the lodge the weekend before opener. Both studious men, they kept a scientific diary and, given all available data, realized their success was determined by one variable: the amount of water in the river, also known as flow rate. Low flows meant good fishing in the spring, and all the other variables were noise. Maybe it really was that simple.

I decided to wade slowly downstream and hunt the flat water for risers. I prefer wading upstream for this, but I was whipped and that other angler was presumably still fishing. And lo, I did find a rising trout. I heard it first, a nice blip on the other side of a log island. I snuck around the log island and got downstream of where I thought the rise was, heard the blip, and found the rings in the evening's silver glare. It was clearly a good fish. It was a trout to make the night.

As I went to throw my first cast, I noticed the portly gentleman who'd been upstream of me was now trucking down the middle of the river, wading through the gloaming silently. I hurried a cast but the guy was closing fast and, because I was tired and in no mood for conversation, I abandoned the rising trout in the side channel and fled. The big guy was right behind me, forty yards at most, an awkward distance. I pushed a bow wave as I waded, flipping glances backward like a bicyclist who knows a semi-truck is soon to pass.

Above the chute, the river bends right before pinching between two cedars and flushing downstream, through the pocket water I'd fished earlier. I decided to bail into the shadows of the cedars on the north bank as a means of stealthy escape. I kept my light off so he wouldn't know I'd left the river, or where I'd gone. Why? I do this sort of thing. I don't know. Then, because I thought I could, I kept the light off as I snuck through the quarter-lit woods, up the big hill with the many fallen trees, and through the oak stand, and entered the jack pines, fly rod still intact. I was huffing and sweating and confused about the night, which had been about one thing, but had become about another.

I crashed into the parking lot. My truck was the only vehicle there.

⌒

Growing up, my favorite farm pond my dad and I fished was called Smith Pond, because Jim and Ginger Smith owned it.

There were two ponds, actually. We always called it Smith Pond, instead of Smith Ponds, or Smiths' Ponds. It was never clear which pond we were talking about. This was before I knew a special place could become an idea.

The Upper Pond was a typical Ohio farm pond, ringed in cattails, and full of fish. We almost always fished it first, like golfers milling around on a putting green.

The Lower Pond was something spectacularly different. Mr. Smith had backed up the little creek at the bottom of a ravine with a thirty-foot earthen dam, and the tannic water had pooled up into the forest and stayed cool and dark beneath the mature canopy. It was a flooded V, deep in the middle, and Mr. Smith—a local tournament angler—had stocked it the old fashioned way: smuggling fish in from other fisheries. This meant there were walleye, flathead catfish, smallmouth, large-mouth, bluegill, and crappie. The walleye existed as rumor. The flatheads I only saw when they sunned themselves like housecats in one of the few sunbeams that touched the pond. The smallmouth would have been mythical if I hadn't caught one of them, a monster, on a fly rod. The largemouth were dark and looked like the Florida bass in my fishing magazines. The crappie and bluegill were enormous. Even the bullfrogs were big enough to cannibalize frog lures . . . a sport that passed the time when the fishing was slow.

The pond was just narrow enough that I could launch a heavy lure to the far side. Still, it was plenty wide enough to keep mystery concealed in the chasm betwixt that bank and your bank. The flooded trees had died, the tops broken off and sunk to the bottom, leaving the skeletal remains standing bleached and firm from the black water. It seemed somehow below the rest of Ohio in a deep and subterranean way.

That lower pond still shimmers from my sleep, thirty years later. I think I'll dream of it until I run out of dreams.

Every once in a while, Mr. Smith would come down trailed by his enormous Rottweiler, Gus, to fish with us. Mr. Smith used an open-faced reel like the pros, and he whipped his cast across the pond, and held the monofilament in his left hand to feel the strikes, and worked the Texas-rig along the bottom, and he'd catch three or four big bass while I watched, star-struck, before inviting us up to the house where Mrs. Smith had made some lemonade. Gus liked to walk next to me. Inside the house, Gus sat next to me while the adults talked. Gus and I were pals. I was pretty heavy into wanting a dog then. And a pond. And to fish Texas-rigged rubber worms like Mr. Smith. But I'd have settled for Gus.

This went on for years, at least in memory. Dad and I would swing by a gas station and load up on Yoo-hoos and beef jerky (both of which I still love), and drive the back way, making a series of right-angle turns across farmland, to the Smith property. I got older but not much better at bass fishing.

Eventually I began taking a fly rod, and Mr. Smith would watch me cast the fly rod and when I caught a bass he'd sort of beam at me and shake his head. He tried casting it once and then handed it to me. There were some big fish caught those years. Bluegill bigger than dad's hand, dark like the last sunset. Every fish was dark there. It was just a dark place cut through summer Ohio.

One spring we showed up and Gus wasn't there. It turned out he'd drowned in the pond that winter, had fallen through too thin ice. Mr. Smith had slid out after him but couldn't get there. Mrs. Smith had watched. I couldn't imagine a sadder thing happening to a dog like Gus or to people like the Smiths. The bottom pond had reached up and snatched that big strong dog and held him down there where those big fish swam like ghosts. It was hard to stare at that pond and think of Gus down there in it. It made it harder to fish it, and I never did cast a Texas-rig worm anywhere near where Gus had drowned for fear of snagging a bone or skull. Smith Pond never felt quite the same after that, and its place in my dreams is the same hinterland reserved for cemeteries.

June 4

Some of those things you want as kids, you vow to get them. Dog, boat, depth finder, proper bass gear, a fish tank for pet bass, another dog . . . you remember, when you get older, that you always wanted these things. The bass boat came just last year: a janky deep V I bought off a cop who was in the process of quitting nicotine during our negotiations. It had a depth finder, spot-lock trolling motor, two casting decks, and a 25 HP four-stroke Honda motor. I didn't need a boat, but the exuberance I felt on the drive back home was reminiscent of the exuberance I felt unleashing a cast into the shadows of Smith Pond.

After getting chased from the river by the mysterious angler, and a very busy weekend at the lodge, I was ready for a break. Not just a break from work, but a break from trout: Bassmaster style. I wanted to stand on the deck of my new bass boat and fish drop-shot rigged Senko worms off a particular point on a particular lake on a beautiful May day. Perhaps, after I got my fill of bass, I could find an evening spinner fall on the river somewhere. These are the sorts of ambitious plans, wedged on top of a normal workday, that have aged me a few years. It's not the work. It's the play.

The bass lake I wanted to fish, which must go unnamed, is actually considered a trout lake. The bass are wild. The trout are stocked, but in Michigan, if a lake has a trout in it, than it's often classified as a trout lake. Driving to the lake, I'd never much considered it for anything other than bass. Trout, to me, are in rivers. You fly-fish for them. Bass live in lakes. You spin fish for them. Unless it's evening poppers, when the fly rod makes more sense. Anyway, it's a trout lake that I consider a bass lake. It was late May. I figured maybe a few bass would be staged off the spawning sand. Maybe I'd find a big smallmouth. Maybe I'd just find a nice easy day of barefoot bass fishing from my boat with my spinning gear. Yes, there was nostalgia involved in my going bass fishing, a reconnection to Smith pond and Ohio summers. One reason, perhaps the best reason, to start a kid in fishing is that fishing will remain a portal to their youth. I'm told that nostalgia is a form of self-harm, but to me nostalgia functions much the same as an oral tradition, a way to feel, as an adult, the joy one felt as a child.

I was rigged up for bass. I was in a bass mindset. Everything that day was meant to be bass, bass, bass . . . but my bass focus wavered almost immediately once I was on the water. While motoring over to a nice cut on the north side of a sand point, I saw a school of very large trout. A stillwater trout is to a bass what a missile is to a bomb. Their trout-y shadows morphed with the terrain of the shallow sand bottom. They were high in the water. They spooked, and shot into a local- ized blob of shadow formed by a passing cloud, a new form of shade I'd never considered before. Then I saw a rise, another,

another . . . this was a single trout, feeding down the line where the wind had blown a bunch of bugs into a small bay. Anglers unceremoniously refer to this as a scum line.

I love bass fishing. But this, *this* was trout water.

I motored back to the dock, pushing the no-wake designation, and grabbed the five-weight and my sling from my vehicle, and motored back across the lake to the sand point. I rigged a dry fly, attached 6x to the hook bend, and added a caddis larva about eighteen inches below it. I have very little experience fishing stillwater trout. But this looked familiar enough: the trout were rising, roaming around in packs through the clear-green water. One pack swam too close to the boat, spooked, skittered for fifty feet, slowed, and then resumed feeding. I stood tall above them in the boat. They darted through the big aquarium water like mutated reflections of nighthawks zipping through a mayfly swarm. To hell with the bass.

My first cast was toward a group of three trout hunting left to right. I picked the shallowest one, which was also in the lead, and let loose a long cast about twenty feet in front of it. The trout swam right to the fly and ate the dropper, dragging the dry fly with it. The adrenaline! I reared back and broke my tippet, left the hook in the trout, and felt a different sort of recognizable nostalgia: I'd messed it up again.

∽

I got it down after that.

The trick with the lake was the following: a small caddis pupa, without bead, fished thirty inches below a dry fly on 6x fluorocarbon, on a long cast. One did not have to cast at a particular trout. You could. I did. But it wasn't necessary. Simply find the most traveled path of the trout, lob a cast into the path, and wait. The trout would come. They would eat. And when they did, I learned the most important lesson at that lake: *Do not set the hook.* Instead, hold the line tight and, in their panic, the trout would set the hook for me.

Those trout sped across the lake like they'd just been let loose from a live trap.

One leapt repeatedly, an absurd amount, ten times at least, as silver and acrobatic as a ladyfish, as a pontoon full of elderly people puttered by. The people raised their wine glasses to me and I pumped a fist. That trout could not be revived and I unremorsefully stashed it in the live well for dinner that night.

Nearing dusk, more pontoons unmoored from the lakeside docks and began to cruise the lake. In the small community of this lake, I believe these are called "wine tours." They cruise the three bays, and drink wine, and enjoy the sunset. It seemed choreographed and I, usually desperate for solitude, enjoyed the company of these quiet retirees on their quiet lake. My reel screamed somewhat obnoxiously—louder, I thought, than their motors. Every time a pontoon passed me on their three-bay tour, they would raise their wine glasses and I, almost perpetually hooked to a big rainbow, would pump my fist. They drank a lot of wine. I pumped a lot of fist.

I didn't think about bass. Not once.

The largest trout was twenty inches and beautiful, the rest an inch or two smaller. It would be too much to ask for them to be wild. They weren't. The lake had no feeder stream, no gravel for these rainbows to spawn on, to connect themselves to their future. They were hatched in a cement room at a state fish hatchery, raised on pellets, transported by truck, and dumped into this lake. A stocked trout is to a wild trout what sports are to real life. The excitement is real, but you have squint at it to keep the big picture from ruining it for you.

The first mayfly spinners were landing on the lake. The sun was setting. It was damn fun, but . . .

I reeled in, waved farewell to the half-dozen touring pontoons, and puttered myself across the lake. Wild trout it was.

⁓

I unhooked the boat at home, forgot about the trout in the live well, blew the family a secret kiss (going inside would have set the kids to begging for me to stay), and left without them knowing I'd been home. The sun was in the trees already. I careened back to M-72. Headed east. Dad was on the hunt.

⌇

The Lab used to have another name, but now we call it The Lab. This is because there's a high bank that looks down into a glass-smooth run on the Au Sable and, on the right day, you can see the trout morphing in and out of the cobbled bottom. A familiar crew was already at the river when I pulled in: John, our breakfast cook at the lodge; Kim, who showed up to the lodge as the sister of a customer and never left the lodge or fly-fishing; and Lance, a photographer and fly tyer who was up for the summer to work in the shop and do some fishing between photography gigs. I asked if it was okay to join and they seemed okay with it, or at least they offered me a warm beer. Four is a lot for an evening of fishing but there were trails in both directions along the river and it would be easy to get away from each other. We rigged up, chitchatting excitedly because it was a perfect May evening—sunny and calm and cooling—and it seemed the trout would rise. Already, through the pine boughs, we could see a mix of different mayfly spinners in the fragmented sun. I shared a few select stories from my afternoon on the trout lake, just enough to wonder if I'd said too much. It was time to go fishing.

We scattered through the woods to our preferred positions. I had requested to have the Big Pine Hole upstream and so that's the direction I went, climbing the pine-straw ridge and then walking along the rim of the valley, the river dark in the shadows but red like blood in the water where the sun hit it. The river, the valley, the world, *was alive*. The sudden fecundity stung me. This was a world without an end, an infinite of somethingness. The mayflies danced freely. Stoneflies drew lines through them. The whitish caddis pushed upstream. Even from up high I could see the splash rises of trout in the bubble lines. Winter was finally gone.

The river was high still, almost too high for the run I'd chosen to fish. I'd thought the tail-out—the slow end of a river pool—might be slow enough for the fish to feed in, but it wasn't. The first good rising trout was directly under the namesake big white pine, rising in a small mid-stream eddy behind a bent stick. I tried the brown bug over the fish and got ignored. Then I tried the sulphur and it ignored that as well. Finally I tried the yellow stone and wasn't ignored. I set the hook and it dogged deep. Oh my! I thought it was a massive fish but it wasn't. Instead, it was a sixteen-inch fish hooked beneath the jaw.

I moved up into the head of the run, which is defined by

an inside bubble line, which bobs on the chop of two dramatically different currents colliding. In this chop there were big trout rolling and rising and chomping as if there were larger mayflies—brown drakes or *Isonychia*—already on the water. I knew they weren't drakes. Drakes don't arrive in secret. But *Isonychia* can hatch unseen in a riffle, the only evidence being the trout slashing and exploding as if the river bottom were on fire.

I tied on a larger brown bug—the size 12—and landed three dandy trout, the biggest perhaps pushing twenty inches, but it was hard to tell in the melee. The water was high and somewhere I'd shipped my waders. I couldn't remember where or when it had happened. How could I be soaking wet and have no recollection of falling in or wading too deep? It didn't seem possible that it had happened, but I was soaked from the chest down. I was soaked to my shoulders. There was water sloshing in the feet of my waders. Somehow, in the mad rush of the day—this perfect day—I'd fallen into 60-degree water and not noticed.

The night pulled closed. Just like that. Just like it does in the early summer, before the drakes and hex begin to hatch, and blur the lines between this world and the other.

I followed my flashlight beam up to the ridge, and through the pines, and back to where we'd parked. The other anglers came along a little later, their lights weaving through the forest. We shared our trout stories loudly and excitedly while removing our waders and our accessories. Lance and John had each landed a nice fish, and Kim had missed one. I put a coat over my wet shirt. We cracked more warm beers, sat on our various tailgates.

We were talking quietly when we heard an owl hoot and a rabbit start screaming. Then we heard the rabbit screaming from a tree, for a moment. It seemed the rabbit was fifty feet in the air! Then an owl (Same? Different? Was it even an owl?) landed in a tree over our heads. Finally all was silent. Had the owl flown the rabbit into the tree? It sounded like it. Had it dropped the rabbit? We hadn't heard anything fall. We discussed. Then we started talking about spooky things because of the owl and the rabbit.

I told the story from before the weekend without embellishment. A large man had seemingly sprinted down the river without a sound, and I'd escaped into the woods to avoid his path. I told them about how I'd been the only car in the parking lot. About how he was a man from nowhere, who had simply appeared upstream of me and disappeared back into the river.

"Indian skin-walker, dude," Lance said immediately, and with great certainty.

"What's that?" I said.

"It's an Indian skin-walker," he said again. "A ghost. At some point in the future, he'll turn into a wolf and devour you."

"Great," I said. "Well, I guess we all have that wolf coming for us."

"Yeah," Lance said. "But that one is yours."

That night—late, too late—I remembered, in a panic, the trout in the live well. I ran outside and found it still firm and cold in an inch of the water that hadn't drained.

I prepared it slowly, slitting the soft white belly and letting the bright innards spill out onto the white cutting board. Katy and I had some wine. The kids were asleep. We didn't talk about much, really, just the day, the week. The windows were open and the night air seeped in. I rolled the trout in flour and blackening seasoning and seared it in butter in the cast iron skillet. I told Katy about the wolf that was coming for me. She said that she'd keep a lookout. I told her that the wolf would appear as a portly well-dressed angler who forgot his glasses. She said she knew lots of such people. But only one, I said, would turn into a wolf. I told her about how I'd experienced several small but distinct metamorphoses. "Things keep starting as one thing, but ending up as another," I told her. "For instance, I meant to write out the orders tonight, and instead I'm soaked with river water."

"Sounds normal to me," she said.

"Perhaps."

She asked about the secret lake from which this trout had been removed, and I told her. Then I told her about when Terry took me to a different trout lake.

Many years ago, he'd taken me to a lake one county over. I met him at his house on a nasty November day. He loaded up the spin rods and we left toward the lake. On the way, he told me all about the lake. How he'd been there last week and fished spawn from the beach and had caught trout just off the drop-off. His car heater baked me to sleepiness. Then his story transitioned to the snowblower he had when he lived in the UP. How it could throw snow thirty feet into the woods. That was real snow, he said. Which is why he drove this big truck. But this truck, he said, was no good and he'd never buy another one and there was no need, he said, for such a big truck in this area of the state, because there wasn't enough snow. His words were like dreams I didn't have to be asleep to see. It was so terribly hot in the truck with the heater on full blast.

We arrived at the lake and we put on our waders, because we had to wade out to cast, he said, and he grabbed the rods. Then he put the rods back in his truck.

"No bait," he said.

"Huh?"

"I forgot the bait," he said. He undid his waders—the big camo neoprene type. He shrugged. Ha! "Can't fish without it."

"So now what?"

"Time to go home."

On the way home he had to stop for something (for his greenhouse, I think) at the hardware store. Our fishing trip had changed into a trip—a successful trip—to the hardware store. On the way back, he talked to me about his greenhouse and I asked a few questions, and, by the end of the our little mini-afternoon together, I thought how nice it would be to one day have a little garden.

"And now you got the garden," Katy said.

That trout from the secret trout lake had flesh as orange as a river sunrise. As I plated it, my Montana poet friend texted me out of the blue, at least six months since the last time we'd spoken. I know him as, among other things, incredibly, perhaps miraculously, prescient. This time, over the surprise trout, I looked at my phone and read it aloud.

When you were sixteen, did you still think you'd be watching the river like this? Sweet life, eh?

CHAPTER 3: TIME IS VERTICAL (OR, HOW I FOUND LAST CHANCE REDEMPTION)

Truth Is Stranger than Fishin'

—1955 book by Beatrice Cook, referenced by
Richard Brautigan in *Trout Fishing in America*

June 6

There's a stretch of the Au Sable I call the Henry's Fork. And somewhere near the end of this chapter, after some time-traveling, I'll return to this stretch of the Au Sable, and I'll catch some fish from it. I know this will happen, because I just caught the trout about a half-hour ago. The catching of these particular trout redeemed something I didn't know needed redeeming.

⌇

The original Henry's Fork is on the Snake River in Idaho. It has several famous stretches for trout fishing, but the most famous is the flatwater section around the town of Last Chance. I visited the Henry's Fork with my family when I was a young teenager and I don't remember much about the town or the geography of the area . . . but that water! That water etched a healthy river-shaped scar into my dream maker. The Henry's Fork is a reflective sheet of moving water with a tangle of currents produced by the tangle of weeds on the bottom which, in turn, produce a ton of insects to feed a bunch of big rainbow trout that are difficult to catch because of the tangles of weeds and currents—to most fly anglers, this circularity is perfection.

We went into Henry's Fork Anglers, the local fly shop, and Mike Lawson was there. Supposedly, he used to tie flies for Cal Gates, who founded Gates Lodge some fifty years ago. René Harrop, another Last Chance legend, also supposedly tied for Cal Gates. So I guess that Last Chance is a trout town with Au Sable roots. In a way I'm about to explain, I ultimately came to the Au Sable with a few Last Chance roots.

Years ago, in some rental place on some summer trip, my dad started laughing wildly in the other room and I went in to investigate. I asked him what he was laughing at, and he said it was this book, *Trout Bum*, by this guy John Gierach, and he was talking about "voidophobia—the fear of empty vest pockets." Gierach not only led us to the Henry's Fork, but he led me to Richard Brautigan's *Trout Fishing in America*—via a single mention, one sentence in one of his books—and thus began an academic acceleration that burned brightly and then faded, gently, like one of many meteors, this book undoubtedly being nothing more than the afterglow.

I love all sorts of rivers, but I'd find, in my one evening on the Henry's Fork, the ideal trout stream, in the platonic sense. The flat clear water and the green waving weeds and the hatches of trout flies: that transparent world that is both stationary and moving. It must have wild trout. It must soothe you with its challenge. Only few rivers can do this. Henry's Fork. Hat Creek. The Firehole. Eventually, the Au Sable. I'm talking about an instant idea: a complicated message that the mind distills instantly into an emotive response. Love is instant, I think. It's instant. I was pulling darts out of a dartboard when Katy walked into the college house I rented with three buddies. I turned, darts in my hand, and knew we were kindred. Rivers don't do *that* to me. But a beautiful piece of Spring Creek, with its transparency and richness and wild trout, with its history and stories, and above all with its mystery, puts me back in my childhood bed, a kid reading by flashlight, a kid with a book that is blowing his mind.

Even though I was a teenager, I remember my only evening on the Idaho Henry's Fork so vividly because it was the perfect evening on what Gierach had described as the perfect trout river. Setting sun, gold living in the chaff on the grass tips, and glowing caddis hatching by the thousands. There were other anglers scattered around the river, but the scale was different. You'd see a guy and you'd think, man, we're awfully close to that guy, and then you'd realize he was not only a hundred yards away, but he was locked into a trout-sized target, elbow bent, line darting, darting, and dropping with a snake-wiggle of the rod tip. He was both right there (I could see him) and not there at all (he had no idea I was there). All the people fishing the Henry's Fork were similarly occupied. These guys were like a bunch of scientists stooped at their respective microscopes. Nothing mattered to them beyond what they were doing. It was a study in existentialism.

I tied on a Dave's Hopper and worked my way up one of those glowing grass banks because that's what you did on other western rivers, caddis hatch or not. My dad found a pod of risers that turned out to be whitefish and even they were tricky for him. I did diddly-squat and didn't think I saw a fish rise.

There were so many caddis that if you didn't know better you'd think the river had some kind of infection. The surface was a mat of shucks. When I walked through the bank grass, the adults flew, fairy-like, around me. They didn't hide the setting sun but magnified it, carrying the light with them, spreading it around the valley, until you were surrounded by light and the soft wings of caddis. I searched vainly for a rising trout. The river seemed dead. Indifferent. Those other anglers . . . they were catching some trout. It was like walking into a familiar, local restaurant and everyone is speaking French. It was a trout river. Trout were being caught. The hatch was happening. Yet, I couldn't raise a trout.

That's it. That's all that happened.

That night, there was a tornado or wind shear. The sky turned green—even at night, it turned green—and the hail pounded the little cabin we'd rented. When the hail began falling, Dad opened the door and stood there with that big green night sky beyond him and white hail streaking through the outside light and clattering on the porch. I was on my knees playing a board game with my mom and sister. Then he closed the door. We heard a train pass by that wasn't a train. The morning was beautiful but a few of the trees around the cabin had fallen down.

⌒

I was a boy of too many interests, but most of my youth was spent at either a golf course or a fishing spot. I left so many divots in our sliver of a front yard you would have thought the lawn had been sold to a sod farm, one 7-iron scoop at a time. I practiced my fly cast by flinging a knotted fly line to the grooves between the rocks that lined our driveway. The knots would get stuck in the grooves, and I'd play-fight a trout on the old Cortland fiberglass rod and Pflueger reel my dad had gifted me, walking backward to make the crappy reel spin drag. I'd bow the rod when the fish jumped like old Flip Pallot did on the *Walker's Cay Chronicles*—the Saturday morning fishing show my dad and I watched together religiously. This imaginary driveway fishing would go on for hours. I could really hit those grooves with that old Cortland rod.

My parents were both teachers and we took stupendous summer vacations across the country, driving a succession of Dodge Caravans, each transmission shittier than the last. My dad drove a Grand Caravan like a long-haul trucker operating without weigh stations or travel logs. We drove—*drove*—to the forty-nine states one can drive to, including Alaska. We also drove to British Columbia, Saskatchewan (*Owls in the Family*, by Farley Mowat, propelled me across that gopher-filled prairie), Manitoba, Ontario, Quebec, Nova Scotia, and took a boat to Newfoundland. My sister and I read countless books in the back of the van. My mom would bury herself in Tony Hillerman novels. My dad just drove.

My schoolmates liked to refer to Ohio as the armpit of America, and it was hard to argue when you were placed in the front of a raft on the Snake River, instructed by the guide not to fall out, and then rowed toward the first good bank. *There's lots of good banks*, the guide kept saying. I used my trusty Cortland fiberglass and knotted fly line to pitch an ostentatious dry fly called a Humpy at the bubble lines coming off the willows. The cutthroats were dumb, big to me, and, once hooked, twisted in the green-clear depths in the shadow of the Tetons. Ohio seemed a penance one must pay to earn such vacations. A Midwestern sentiment if ever there was one. But I couldn't shake trout—the idea of them—from my mind. They seemed uneclipsable by anything else on earth: too bright to be totally obscured by, or from, the rest of my life.

The night after a full day of western trout fishing, I'd lie, sunburnt and warm, and feel the rocking of the boat in my body. Near sleep, my fly would float across the darkness. A rise! I'd set, then wake up, right arm above me, lost in purpose.

We saw, and fished, a lot of famous rivers that way. But the Idaho Henry's Fork, in some way, is the center river of this meandering western reverie, even if I only fished it for two hours and didn't catch a thing. The Henry's Fork brought to life the stories I'd read in the fly-fishing magazines. It offered a benchmark for what a *great* trout river looked like, what a cloud of caddis truly was. I could only think of the scene as a sort of natural excellence. The Henry's Fork of Idaho, from

Gierach's stories to my youthful humbling, certainly laid the foundation for a later love of the Au Sable. But it isn't my home water. And neither, after all these years, is the Au Sable.

My home waters flow through Smoky Mountain National Park in Tennessee and North Carolina. These are foamy white, plunging rivers that fill the air with mist before settling into deep prismatic pools. They are my home waters because they were the nearest wild trout waters to where I grew up in Ohio. Before I fished across the American West—before the Firehole and the Henry's Fork—the clear mountain streams of the Appalachians were what I thought of when I thought of trout water.

The first trout I ever caught on a fly was from the Little River in the Great Smoky Mountain National Park when I was six years old. It was a small rainbow that took a wet fly. My fly line was white and the trout was by a large boulder, and I'll bet it was Columbus Day weekend in October—the first good vacation in the new school year.

Back then we stayed at a hotel in Gatlinburg that had private porches overlooking a small trout stream, which flowed not just next to the hotel, but along it: the wall of the hotel was the bank of the stream. When we'd arrive late on a Friday night I would go to the porch to be just that much closer to trout water. Before sleep I could feel the small force of the current in the bones of the hotel.

If the Henry's Fork would later represent an ideal to the trout fisher in me, the Smoky Mountains, with their sweet winds and clear rushing waters and salamanders, rhododendrons, jewel-bright (and often jewel-small) trout, were nonetheless pure homespun magic: a tingling ghost story, or a game-winning home run.

Even after I outgrew the family vacations and got into college and its trappings, and Michigan fly-fishing and whatnot, I still returned to the Smokies, now dragging friends. In college, two buddies and I put a pond-rowboat in the back of a pickup and drove all the way down to the south-side of the Smokies, to Fontana Lake in North Carolina specifically, launched into a rainstorm, and spent three hours rowing across the lake to arrive at Hazel Creek to fish in the footsteps of the great nature-lover and writer Harry Middleton. The old boys at the marina stood and watched us row. We must have rowed ten minutes before they hollered, as we were still well within earshot, *you sure you don't want to rent a <u>motor</u>boat?*

Yep. We're sure.

We made it. I'd forgotten a rain jacket so I wore a parka I fashioned from a garbage bag. We set up our slouching tents in the rain and shivered our way through the night. The next morning was sunny and beautiful. That evening I hooked an enormous rainbow trout from the base of a swollen waterfall. Given its unusually large size, the trout was likely a lake fish that was in the river to spawn. It ran into the falls, far beneath them, before turning course and sprinting downstream, stripping line from the reel and then stripping the fly from the tippet.

The next year, this girl Katy and I took a quick vacation to the Smokies. It was a place that I wanted to show her, even if she'd been there several times with her own family. We camped along Deep Creek in a backcountry site. I caught two small trout from a pinch point between two boulders, both on a Prince Nymph. Katy and I were pretty young then. Neither of us really saw the path forward. We'd met at the perfect time, each of us coming off all-time lows. She'd been transferring colleges trying to get it right, and I'd nearly failed out of college if for no reason other than to scare myself. The son of two teachers, it's funny that failing out of college was the worst thing I could imagine. But I didn't feel right in the head. The world was too big. The world in which I felt comfortable was beginning to feel pretty small.

The day we hiked out of Deep Creek was beautiful, near seventy degrees, and we stopped at a small pass over Deep Creek and watched two trout surface feed in the pool below. They were nice trout, browns, each over a foot long. They held high in that clear mountain water. Trout may not feel emotion like we do, but I think they can be happy, and Katy and I somehow knew that we could be too.

Fourteen years went by. After one tragedy, we emerged with two boys. After another tragedy, we emerged with a fly-fishing lodge. We got whisked up into busyness. It wasn't until the kids were properly in grade school that we were able to consider a vacation. It was wintertime . . . and we craved the mountains. And in writing about the section of the Au Sable that reminds me of the Henry's Fork—what I'd meant to be a straightforward entry into my 2019 fishing journal—I found notes from that first trip with our children saved on the desktop of the computer, which is what prompted this current digression.

A SMOKY MOUNTAIN JOURNAL

February 22

Holden is seven years old and he likes to fish. If you ask what he wants to be when he grows up, he'll shrug and say, "Probably a guide" with the same fatalism as the son of a farmer or miner. I'll never forget that first trout I caught on a fly. His happened so long ago, he's long since forgotten. Fly-fishing was time I spent with my dad. For him, fly-fishing usually means time that Dad is away.

When we arrive in the park the rivers are high, fast, clear, cold. The weather is warm and the snow is gone. There are stoneflies hatching, but there are no rising trout. The right rig is a nymph rig. It's hard work for a dry-fly kid. We try a lot of seemingly "perfect" pools. But there are no perfect pools when you're seven years old, fishing a swollen mountain river. A run on Abrams Creek would be nice if it weren't for a log at the end of the drift that the boy cannot avoid. When he snags, he looks about, distracted.

"Go on," I say.

He happily leaves the river to climb in the rhododendron with his brother, Aaron, who we've nicknamed Double-A after the battery, while I fish. Later, I see him crouched in the jungle, photographing me.

"Hey Dad, Dad," he says. He often says things in double, presuming I'll ignore the first.

"Yeah?"

I hear the shutter close about twenty times.

We find other perfect pools that are impossible for him to fish: too deep, or with an overhang, or the drift is beyond his reach. We try the lower Little River where I surprisingly run into a friend/client from Michigan who reports that he'd just accidentally caught a hellbender salamander on a nymph. The boys stare at the phone picture of it, spellbound. Then, later that day, they hunt tirelessly for hellbender salamanders while I pool hop, picking up a few trout along the way, one of which I drop while trying to show Double-A, who is four and outgoing, vociferous, profane.

"Ah shit," he says. "That's okay."

February 24

I'm not too old to look for salamanders, to climb trees, to boulder hop; but only a kid can do it like a kid. I watch them as if I'm watching myself. Holden, always contemplative, asks a series of specific questions. Then, once they are answered, grabs a branch, holds it like a rifle, and starts sneaking through the riverside rhododendron jungle as if on special assignment. "C'mon army!" he calls, the army being Double-A. I fish. Later, Holden appears near the river, anxious to join me. He flips the indicator rig upstream, mends, watches. He does this a half-dozen times. Hands me back the rod.

"I really want you to catch one," I say. "But it's tough."

"Is it really, really, really tough?" Holden says, like he does.

"Very."

The weather that week is so perfect there is no distinction between days—every day is sunny, beautiful, warm. The boys' bodies fill with bruises from the boulders, the tree climbing. The tip of my thumb is rough from fish teeth, my right knee is bruised from a fall. Katy soldiers on, up one mountain and down another, commanding the boys, "Once I start hiking I don't stop. Move it!" and they run on ahead.

We hike to Abrams Falls where, along the way, I have the best day I've ever had in the Great Smoky Mountains National Park. A day of so many rainbows, including some big ones, that I quit in midstream, say enough is enough, and make the terrific mistake of trying to hike out of the river in the middle of the famous, or infamous, Horseshoe. It's a decision that leads to an hour-long hike through an ensnaring nest of thorny vines and interwoven rhododendron. Back at the car, the boys are without shirts or shoes. They are running around the downstream edge of Cades Cove. Katy is sitting on the tailgate. I'm soaked in sweat, bleeding, bruised. She hands me the water bottle. The mountains have taken control of the schedule.

February 27

This afternoon we drive up to Elkmont, a fast section of the Little River where an old neighborhood of leased houses had been abandoned. The boys take their metal detectors and go "detectin'," as Double-A says, around the old houses. I take my fly rod and head down to a pool where, nearly twenty years earlier, I lay on my belly face-first on a steep cliff and watched a Quill Gordon rise as a nymph, attach to the surface film, bust out of its shuck, and get eaten by a small brown trout.

Nothing today.

I push upstream and Holden catches up to me and says he wants to fish. Once again the river is impossible for him to wade. We fish off an old stone deck that was once attached to one of the houses. There are some danger-ously overhanging branches, and stuck in them are not one but two Squirmy Wormies.

It is another difficult situation. It's a fast, deep, plunge pool. The boy has to flip the line downstream, load cast away from the overhanging branches, and then roll the rig into the pool.

I'm thinking of all my dad went through—when Holden hooks a trout.

It's a small suicidal rainbow that takes the fly when it is hanging there, and hooks itself. The fish is quickly corralled—there's not much fight in a six-inch trout. Holden flips the trout toward his hand, just like they do on the YouTube fishing videos he watches. It's an aggressive strategy and I catch the fish in midair before it flies into the woods behind us. As I unhook the trout, Holden leaps victoriously. It is easy to underestimate the weight my expectations have on my kids. Katy and Double-A come over to observe, and the releasing of the trout is a family event.

I fish up the river some more, Holden hopping along with me, the big camera in his hands. He keeps a careful eye on my lack of success, records it with digital image. Finally I quit and wade to him.

"You done?" he says, as if we've been fighting.

"Finished," I say.

"I caught more fish than you," he says, camera pointed on me, shutter clicking.

Asking for directions at our hotel, the woman at the front desk struggles to describe to me the distance between two points. I can't grasp it. How could it be fifteen minutes from one point, and an hour from a similar distance but different starting point? Finally, frustrated but polite, she says, "Because of a mountain." She pauses. "Around here, sweetie, time is vertical."

February 28

The last evening of the trip, we drive around the park. The boys pepper me with questions and I answer, and elaborate. I tell them about each pool. The big rock where my dad tight-lined a nymph and caught an eighteen-inch brown that we both knew had to live under that rock. The pull-off we loved near Metcalf Bottoms. The Looking Glass pool where we used to watch the trout feed, but could never catch them.

I feel a spectacular, fleeting, even silly moment of ownership, as if they are my rivers, my mountains. The questions quit. The boys fall asleep. Katy too. I'm just about to drive out of the park and back to where we're staying . . . but I think better of it. I U-turn by the national park sign and keep driving, the way we came, through the last of the daylight.

I open the window, feel the cold breath of Little River. Its cataracts flash white through the trees, bright and alive, and loud, loud with life.

Now that's trout water, I whisper.

∽

Trout water.

I first saw the Au Sable during a white miller hatch in late August. The white miller is a fluttery moth-y type caddis that sweeps across the river at dusk and is of only passing interest to trout. I'm sure the hundreds of trout we saw rise were eating the fly formerly known as *Pseudocloeon*, which is a microscopic blue-winged olive that falls, en masse, in the evening to lay its even more microscopic eggs. It's a classic masking hatch: a very noticeable fly masking the existence of a more diminutive, and often more abundant, second fly that the trout are actually feeding on. In magic, this is sleight of hand. And anybody who hunts and fishes knows that nature is a trickster. I fished a big elk hair caddis and caught a few, bright, brook trout that were too young to care that my fly was wrong.

The Au Sable, I've learned, is a perpetual beguiler. For every secret serum discovered, the river develops a new poison. This, to me, makes it a haunting river. In the daylight, in the summer, it is flat and clear and the bottom waves with thin green weeds and the rocks are brick-colored and the sand is soft and clean and worn into waves on the bottom. The small trout dart about, from sun to shadow. It has history and culture, and it has solitude and moods. It fishes well at night, when you can't see. It can crush your soul if you care too much about catching trout. But when it is alive, it is so alive. It's the brilliant but bipolar friend: you hang in there for the brilliance.

In the mid-1990s, my parents were looking for a cabin on a river. And swallowing my love of the Smokies, and the unreality of a cabin on the Henry's Fork, I gave my fifteen-year-old vote in such a way that they knew years of spoiling me would guarantee ample and indefinite teenage moroseness should they pick a summerhouse elsewhere. The FOR SALE sign was removed. I began tying flies for the quiet owner of Gates Lodge. I waded the river in front of the cabin, up and down, falling in love.

The Au Sable, with its confused but flat currents, fecundity, and mystery, is a Henry's Fork–type of river. And within the Au Sable, there are stretches that I consider particularly Henry's Fork-y. And within those spots, there's one spot that is most Henry's Fork-y. And it's this spot that I think of as the Henry's Fork of the Au Sable: the river fading out of a riffle into a vast, shallow run, the currents swirled by underwater weeds, and the banks—well, one bank at least—haired in long grasses with seed pods that, in the dusk, hold the light of the setting sun. It's far downriver of my parents' cabin, in what I call the middle river, somewhat near a cabin I joint-own with a few other guys, a little trout hideaway that is almost, but not quite, in the right spot.

Speaking of the cabin . . . In one of those odd circles one finds in fly-fishing, John Gierach actually stayed at the cabin a few years after we got it. John Gierach is about as famous as you can get in fly-fishing, so being in a remote cabin on a famous river was probably a good thing for him. Of course, while he was there, the hot water heater broke in the cabin and he and his buddy were stuck taking cold showers.

While the Au Sable is a public river, getting foot access to the Henry's Fork of the Au Sable was, until, recently impossible. I don't trespass, and while I'm in a position to receive a lot of trespass rights, I rarely use them for several reasons: I always think that the landowners will forget they gave me permission, and I tend to fish late at night, and the beam of my flashlight through a bedroom window at 1:00 a.m. probably isn't what most landowners had in mind when they said, *Come fish here any time you want.* So I had resigned myself to visiting this small section of water by boat, until just a few days earlier, when good fortune walked through the fly shop door.

It was busy in the shop—June is peak season—when a man introduced himself and revealed that he owned a property that seemed, by his description, to be near our cabin and even nearer to the Henry's Fork of the Au Sable. He wanted to use his tractor to fill in some potholes and needed to scoop the dirt from our property and move it to his property. "Fine," I said. "I'll talk to the other guys." I paused before going on. "Say," I said. "Would you think it would be much of a trouble if I could walk across your property and downstream to do a little trout fishing?" It wasn't clever and I think he saw it coming, but at least he agreed. He got the dirt. I got the fishing spot.

∽

The problem us anglers have is that we rarely see what is truly happening. What we see, instead, is what we believe is truly happening. Our minds are a dam between our eyes and our brain. We see only what we believe is there. Prejudice invades our sight and makes us blind to these secret trout feeding in the shadows of our overconfidence (even if all we *know* is that nothing is rising). This is a lesson I should have learned many years ago on the Henry's Fork, when I was too busy casting my grasshopper to look for the bulging rises of trout eating the caddis.

Years later, Rusty taught us teenagers to sit on the bank and just watch the river come to life. Be a bank beaver, he said. So we did. We sat on the bank and we watched the river. He was right. The river did come into focus. What looked to be a dead pool was secretly alive, what looked to be a lost night was found in the quiet rings that we almost didn't notice.

I sat on the bank of the Henry's Fork of the Au Sable earlier this evening, and I watched the river come into focus . . .

The slanting sun shone down river, and in pine-splintered beams I could see dancing mayflies. They were Borcher's Drakes, or, in Latin, the *Leptophlebia*. The *Leptophlebia* hatches by crawling out onto the bank, and, not surprisingly, the duns —or adults—are a non-entity to the fly fisher because they are rarely if ever on the water. It's the spinners that captivate the trout and the angler, because any mayfly that wishes perpetuity must, at some point, lay eggs on the water. The spinners dance high, in localized clouds. After mating, they plummet from thirty feet or more, and land on the water in the sort of uncomfortable-looking positions you'd see beneath an amateur trapeze act. Often you can't even see the *Leptophlebia* spinners in the air. They just appear on the water as if scattered by a trout god.

Just to the south a towering cloudbank burned with the falling sun . . .

The river here is wide: a slow spilled-out riffle flowing over weed patches and pebbled pockets, waist-deep, and in the evening it is sheened by the sunset reflection. The first rise, when I saw it, was not a rise at all. It was a trout head. I stared into a bubble line and saw a trout head poke out of it. I even saw its eye! I stared at where I saw the head, and then I saw a second trout head poke up between me and the first trout head. Wham! Just like that, there were trout heads everywhere. They looked like gopher heads poking out of Farley Mowat's Saskatchewan prairie. It was the best rise of trout I'd seen so far this spring.

These head-showing trout were seam-shifters. Most trout will follow a single seam, which is a visible line where two river currents meet. To a trout, the seam offers a slow spot to hold position while the two river currents bring them food. So if a seam moves ten feet, which seams do, the trout generally move with the same seam. Generally is the operative word, because these trout did not. They were moving all over the place, switching places, overlapping. It's not that I could see the trout underwater, but they'd rise eight times in a row, like swimmers taking breaths, right across the river, going from thirty to fifty feet away, and then feeding right back toward me.

I shrugged, smiled, and chucked a cast right out among them. I felt like I was throwing a hunk of meat into an alligator pit. Hell, it couldn't be this easy. It wasn't. I had to play around with the drift, figure out that crucial downstream flick of line, what anglers refer to, as a mend or correction (i.e., a fix to keep the fly drifting naturally), and finally, just when I was feeling a bit embarrassed for myself, a lovely trout ate the fly so innocently my embarrassment shifted from me to the trout.

The trout ran across the river and leapt, wild and silver, and I noticed all the heads in the bubble lines stopped (I often look to see if the fish are still rising when I'm fighting a fish, which is greedy but I can't help myself).

She was a blocky chrome rainbow, about eighteen-inches long, thick right to the tail. The Au Sable is not known as a rainbow river because they are generally only found in certain sections; and, I think, because there are a lot more of them now than there used to be, and conventional wisdom tends to lag behind the truth.

I crouched and held the fish in the water. No need for the waders I'd worn. A pair of English rubber boots, those green ones you see in Orvis catalogs, would be fitting. Perhaps my neighbor would let me build a small bench here. I could sit here the rest of the season, pausing from a good book to scan for trout heads in the bubble line.

After releasing the rainbow, only a few heads reappeared. The rest, I figured, had spooked off, though I wondered if they went into hiding or had relocated upstream or downstream, and continued feeding. On the Idaho Henry's Fork, John Gierach quoted Mike Lawson as saying that angling pressure has made the trout move between rises, which makes the trout much more difficult to pinpoint and fool with a fly. I don't know if it's from pressure, but I know this happens on the Au Sable.

The rises became sporadic, so I focused on two trout that were far out in the current and feeding well. The only way I knew they were different fish is that they rose simultaneously. The upper one rose like the rest: just the head. The downstream trout rose with a much less consistent explosion of water. They were mostly in and out of the far seam in the middle of the river.

They rejected the dark stacked hackle spinner—the one with the goose biot—so I gave them John Sheets's Red Quill, a cult-classic on the Au Sable, which has a light body of brown rooster quill. I've noticed some days they like the dark fly, and some days the light fly. But 95 percent of the time, it'll be one of the two. On the first cast the upper trout ate the Sheets spinner. It boiled when I set the hook. There was no screaming run or leap like the previous trout. This was a surface thrashing dogfight with what turned out to be a tired old male rainbow, not snake-thin but with kind of slouchy flesh. He was handsome, though, still in spawning colors, with a bold red stripe. Sometimes I think spawning trout use up all their energy turning so beautiful and that the sex is actually the easy part.

As I dusted the fly and inhaled the bankside scents of mint and pine (and a whiff of victory) the exploding trout exploded, again, far out in the dark river. One more? I looked at the huge cloud bank, which was now as dark and stony and unmoving as a Yosemite monolith. Sure, one more. As I false-cast the trout exploded again. I sprung the rod forward, formed the index and thumb of my left hand into a ring, and let the line shoot through it. I knew the cast was right even if it was too dark to see my fly. Terry always said that sight was overrated when it comes to fly-fishing. You don't need to see the fly, he said. Humans have been hurling pointy things at animals for a really long time. Keep your eyes on the target and let the body do what the body do. This is what archers call instinctual shooting—a form of shooting that, with an arrow, I've always done poorly. Sometimes, with a fly rod, I find redemption.

It was a brown, and it was big. I didn't pull the trout out of the water or bother with a picture. I do remember it was dark-backed and seemed old, a male, slightly hooked jaw, slightly tapered through the belly. When I released him he stayed tight to the bank, finning at my feet. A whip-poor-will sang out. I whistled back.

And I went home.

And I've been writing since.

It's raining now. Spring rain. I've opened the window in my little writing cave and I can hear and smell the rain on the deck. The kids are asleep—I write as they fall asleep in their room next door. If I leave before they are asleep, they will yell at me for leaving and this threat keeps me on task.

Sometimes after I'm done writing I go in and sit by them and think about what they are dreaming about and wonder if it's what I was dreaming about when I was their age. I doubt it is but I hope it feels the same.

CHAPTER 4: FISH AS IF THE UPSTREAM BULL WATCHES

'Tis better to bear the ills we have than
fly to others we know not of.

—WILLIAM SHAKESPEARE, *Hamlet*

June 12

On a float this afternoon, Tank Ron and I found a trout we could never catch up to. It fed its way right up the river, through two big bends separated by a long straightaway. We watched for its rises like we were watching the night sky for meteors, each one simultaneously expected and unexpected. The trout fed right up past another boat, while the dudes in the boat—friends of ours—pasted casts at its afterimage. I poled upstream past their boat, with Tank Ron yelling, "There he is again," as if it were Moby Dick–breaching, which I think confounded the other boat because they pulled anchor and moved off and we remained in pursuit. I was stand-up poling in the back of the boat and giving it all I had to catch up to this trout. It was putting a hundred feet between its rises and Tanker was yelling about it and there were still a few of the big duns on the water and finally . . . I knew we could not catch it. Such a fish: it was uncatchable.

Never. Not unless some lucky neophyte was flailing the water waiting for a fish to swim into his fly and this trout, this highest echelon of uncatchable trout, picked that exact moment—at the end of its hundred-foot submersion—to eat the neophyte's bug. But this, I think, would not count as a catch. Semantics. If I were a trout, that's how I'd rise. I'd think I'd outsmarted them all, only to be caught by a newbie.

I'd actually tried to talk Tanker out of going fishing this morning, as if my resistance to fishing might be mistaken for responsibility. I've got as much a fishing problem as I do any other problem. There are things I don't have because of fishing. My yard, house, all of it looks like it does because I fish. This little spare bedroom in which I write and tie flies looks like a dorm room, albeit a dorm room with several dozen hooks in the carpet and feathers everywhere. Every once in a while I'll find a level of trout-stasis, a singular satisfaction—often following a particularly good evening of fishing—and turn my attention toward adult-type things.

Predictably I relented to Tanker's pestering, and after getting the boat ready and driving across the county, he asked *me* if I thought the fishing would be any good.

"It better be," I told him. "You talked me into it."

"It's fishing," he said, and he had a point. Tank Ron and I met years ago on the South Branch. I was a college kid then, just working in the fly shop, and he was at the National Guard base in Grayling. We just kept running into each other until we decided to fish together. Rusty nicknamed him Tank Ron, but now it's most often just "Tanker."

It was a cold June day, half-sun, north wind, and the leaves were flipped silver as if it were about to rain, but the clouds were thinning. It was 58 degrees at 3:00 p.m., and we were looking for brown drake duns to be hatching in the afternoon because it was unseasonably cold, and brown drakes will sometimes hatch during the afternoon on unseasonably cold days. This was one of those days. There were dozens of drakes on the river. Not hundreds. Not thousands. It wasn't a blanket hatch. It was a trickling hatch down the north bank of the river, where the south sun had warmed the muck *just enough* for a few bugs to hatch and, from our immediate boat-launch observations, a few big trout to eat them.

The somewhat fuzzy plan cleared up right quick. I'd pole the riverboat up the river, and we'd take turns on the big trout that were feeding in the seam along the north bank. The river in this stretch—and many other stretches of Michigan rivers—is lined by weeds and even a few lily pads. Sometimes I don't recognize trout water for trout water. Years ago I mistook this same stretch of river for chub water. But once I saw it for trout water, I began seeing similar water as trout water too. Before I knew it, I was seeking out the type of water I'd once written off.

The river got wider and the promise grew deeper.

⁓

The first fish of the afternoon was cruising a black-muck backwater created by an enormous, ancient log-island. The island split the current into two, the north current flowing along the weeds, the south current joining the main seam. Between the two currents was a tennis court's worth of dead water. That's where a trout was rising. Like many trout in slow water, it was a mover. It moved all over the place. The riverboat wasn't originally designed for such trout—it was designed to move food between logging camps—but the boat has found a second career in trout fishing, as well as, I hope, a measure of immortality.

When the trout rose near us, Tanker threw an across-and-down reach cast and fed slack into the drift. We hadn't discussed the strategy or the boat position, other than me saying, "good," and him nodding. We've fished together for twenty years and the across-and-down reach cast is always how Tank Ron does it. His fly sat stationary in the dead water as the current near the boat sucked his fly-line downstream. The dry fly drift is a postponement of the inevitable.

The trout swirled under his dun but didn't take.

"Refused it!" Tanker pronounced, sounding very much like Terry sounded on the bench: *Refusal!* Well, the two cut their trout teeth on the same waters. We all probably sound the same with our Au Sable lexicon. Tanker collected his line, held his fly between his thumb and index finger, and waited.

The next rise was revelatory. We watched the wings of a brown drake poke suddenly out of the dead water—a fresh hatcher. The trout rose an inch from it.

"That trout just ate the shuck," Tanker said.

"Sure looked like it," I said.

"That trout just ate the *shuck*," Tanker said. He looked back at me, and then at the fish. "I don't tie any shucks."

"Who does?" I said.

Tanker hunched over his fly box and muttered to himself, *no . . . no . . . well? . . . no*. His line was bouncing on the water and every time it touched the water it would produce a delicate little wave of water.

"Snowshoe emerger," Tanker announced, meaning a fly with a wing from the foot of a snowshoe rabbit. He snapped shut his box, knotted on the fly. He squeezed on some silicone fly floatant, blew on the fly, dropped it in the water . . . waiting. That's what you do. You wait on the fish.

I was paddling gently with the big beavertail paddle and it was easy work to hold us in position. The sun was out completely. The trout rose three times going away—the last rise was actually in the far current, the one by the weeds, at least eighty feet from the boat. And then, after a minute or so, it rose near us. I heard the sound of Tanker's line hum through the guides, the soft snap of the fly pausing before the motion of the cast reversed, the water within the fly, unattached to the energy, flung from the materials in a fine, rainbowed mist. As Tanker lengthened his line with each false cast, the little puffs of mist appeared, each further than the last (and closer and closer to the target), until a loop of line shot through the series of fading mist clouds and straightened and fell, steady, silent, perfect.

A foreshadowing wake appeared and then the trout rose, and was hooked.

When the trout was close, I dropped the paddle and slid the net beneath the thrashing fish as we drifted backward. It was a beautiful trout, with a bit of jewelry: it had recently been snagged in the side with a Little Cleo and wore it as a silver adornment. The Little Cleo is a simple lure of bent and polished metal. Typically they have a treble hook, but the conscientious angler had cut off the other two hooks. The line had parted an inch above his knot—a fray in the line, perhaps.

Undoubtedly the trout had swiped at the Little Cleo, and the angler had hooked the trout in the side, doubling its pulling power, and causing the monofilament to snap. Soon, the Little Cleo would be hanging from my visor, next to the jointed Rapala I'd pulled from the side of a big trout I caught further downriver years before on a Hendrickson.

"I don't think it'll go twenty," Tanker said.

⌇

I have to travel back in time twenty years, to New Zealand, to best think about my evening with Tank Ron. I'm thinking of a particular bend in a particular New Zealand river, an uncastrated bull, and a large trout.

It was a meadow river with a public camping hut downstream near a lake. Katy had stayed behind in the hut while I went fishing. The river had appeared fishless for several miles. I'd heard a bellowing bull most of the walk upstream, getting louder as I proceeded, meaning that the distance between myself and the bull was shrinking. I finally saw the bull before I saw any trout, and so I knew my fishing day was soon to end. I slowed my pace, my eyes exploring every rock for the shadow, tail, or even essence of a trout. And then, in the last bend before I reached the bull . . . I found the trout. By that point in our New Zealand visit, I'd learned a lot about New Zealand rivers and their trout. But I knew far less about how to negotiate with bulls.

I'm not sure if trout can sense nervousness but I think they can, and a lesson I learned after a few months in New Zealand was to embrace the processes that precede the first cast to a sighted trout. It began with a slow walk up the river in my river-rotted hiking boots, my gorse-torn polypro tights (for lack of a better word), my splotched Columbia shorts, scanning the clear water for trout-y shadows and shapes and movement. Spotting the trout meant that I stopped moving. Stopping moving is different from freezing. Freezing is a violent action with sharp edges that a trout will spot at a great distance. A seasoned pointing dog doesn't freeze. Instead, the dog performs a series of small actions—each softer than the last—that matriculates quickly into a full-on point. So, upon seeing a trout or the ring of a rise, I'd force myself into a series of softer and softer actions, until I was still. This is why careful waders like Terry were able to get within a rod length of trout while others, though acting sneaky, can never seem to keep a trout on the feed. And keeping a trout on the feed is the fundamental goal of the trout angler.

The difference between a sighted New Zealand trout in the morning of a long summer day, and a big Michigan trout rising to a dwindling hatch of mayflies at dusk is the difference between handing a heart patient some hypertension pills, and administering first aid to someone having a heart attack. That New Zealand trout, I learned, was going to feed, on and off, for the next eight hours. That Michigan trout? Ten minutes. I came to New Zealand with a bit of the desperation Michiganders have when they finally find a big rising fish. Our trout always seem to flash into existence—a rise or two—before fading back into imagination. This is one of the many things that makes Michigan trout fishing seem unfair.

The New Zealand angler has the luxury of time, and after spotting the trout and stopping moving, the next step in my process was to contemplate my depleted box of flies, check knots, and figure out how close I thought the fish would allow me to get. There were considerations of sun, shadow, and wind. Not on how they affected me, but how they affected the fish. I learned to treat each fish as if it might be the last fish I'd see, ever.

It was the angry bull on the South Island meadow river that reinforced the lesson. It remained just one bend upstream, still bellowing, stomping his foot in the tall grass, and letting me know that my fishing for the day ended with the big trout in front of me. Either I'd catch it or I wouldn't, and that would be my day.

The trout was sitting on the outside of a fast bend, in a little cove the current had carved from the bank. It was unmoving. It was not on the bottom. It was not near the surface. All of this was odd. Most New Zealand trout I spotted would be on the insides of the bends, away from the fast water; and, if they weren't spooked, would be wagging their tails and feeding in some fashion. This trout was stock still, held in place in that current by nothing less than trout magic. Perhaps it too was scared of the bull. Or perhaps this was its bedroom, and it was finished feeding for the day. I checked my knots slowly. Replaced tippet. I crouched on one knee and kept one eye on the bull (an all-white marble brute that, in recollection, has grown to resemble the evil doppelganger of Babe the Blue Ox) and one eye on this trout. And as I sat there—after twenty minutes or more—the trout darted into the current and fed. And again. Again. Soon enough, it was on the feed.

But that was only the first step.

The trout, after darting in and out of the current on the outside bank of the bend, just sort of swam away. Well, it darted out, ate a nymph, and swam away. It morphed from a perfectly visible trout into a lean gray shape that moved casually through the fast current before entering the obscuring glare upstream.

(Interestingly, the glare in New Zealand served to hide trout, whereas on the Au Sable, at last light and even into night, the silver glare serves to illuminate the rings of a rising trout. I hunt for glare in Michigan as I hunted against glare in New Zealand, and I think the opposition of these two approaches might be the best way I have to describe the differences of the fishing in each place.)

I went downstream and crossed the riffle and, cursing in fear, walked up the loose rock on the inside of the bend. The bull, witnessing this insubordination, bellowed and flung snot. The light was terrible for sighting, just flat shiny gray, like a skim of milky ice. I had to walk very slowly. More slowly, perhaps, than I'd ever walked a trout stream before. It would be too easy to spook the fish and then, fishless, turn away from the bull and head back . . . defeated, and a coward to boot.

I found the trout at the top of the run, forty yards from the bull. Too close, it seemed. But also, just close enough.

The trout had moved to where it should have been all along: in a foot of water on the shallow inside of the bend. It was feeding in the innermost current, the faintest little trickle, far removed from the main spill of water. It was as happy as a trout could be, darting all around the shallow water, assuming the shapes of rocks, reappearing. I chose to cast to his inside so I didn't have to put the line over him. He'd fed in that direction numerous times, and he seemed quite eager to please.

I worked some line out, my eyes flicking from the trout to bull, and waited for the wind to quit and then fired a cast to his right. He moved over to investigate, and I readied to set the hook . . . and then he twirled, and darted ten feet to the left, and held deeply, unmoving. Fine, I figured, I'll wait him out. And I did. Serenely. I had nowhere else I could go. The bull was now just staring at me and breathing heavily. I could hear the snot rattling in his agitated breaths. Somehow, this was more ominous than the stomping or bellowing. So I decided to keep waiting it out. And, eventually, the trout swam back over to the shallow inside of the bend and began feeding. Changing tactics, I waded out into the fast water and threw to his left and he swam over and ate the nymph as if nothing had been wrong in his whole life.

It was not the biggest fish I caught in New Zealand by length, but by weight it was the greatest. The handle above his tail was too fat for my hand so I beached him on the rocks and pounced to hold him in place. His belly was jagged with the skeletons of what I assumed were mice, as big trout will eat such things. The mice had tried to swim across the river, and, one by one, they'd failed. There wasn't a red spot on that trout. Silver like morning clouds.

I let the trout go and stood and saluted the bull. When I began walking downstream he resumed his bellowing.

⟆

Steadiness comes naturally to some. In others, in me, it just sort of appears and disappears with heartbreaking unpredict-ability. Years ago I sat in a tree stand and shot a nice buck with a bow. I was so excited my vision was starting to go black when I let the arrow fly, but I remained steady and the arrow flew true. Fishing in New Zealand is similar to bow hunting in Michigan, in that any nervous energy you have will, at some point, be telegraphed to your quarry. It could be from freezing suddenly upon sighting a seven-pound brown finning in a long clear glide, or rushing an approach, botching a cast, or firing desperate fly after fly, like increasingly bad pick-up lines, at the trout. None of this works in New Zealand.

The fellow that didn't teach me this was my friend Kyle, though he was originally introduced to me by his last name, Junker, so I began to call him Junker too. We met in the boardroom at the lodge (a sort of communal room) when I was sixteen or seventeen years old. At the time Junker had a buzz cut and was tying flies for Rusty and living in his car on the Au Sable. He spent his winters in New Zealand, living on his fly-tying money. His bankroll had nothing to do with fast tying. It had to do with living in his car and eating Kraft Mac and Cheese—saving a penny can be easier than earning two when it comes to professional fly-tying. We fished some together in Michigan—sometimes a lot together—and his stories of New Zealand I learned by heart, a sort of oral tradition, which fed a fire to go to this mysterious country with the big trout in the clear water. When good fortune sent Katy and me to New Zealand for nearly two years, Junker decided to come too, though separately (he by plane, and Katy and I by ship). After several misadventures—boats, cars, maps—we were reunited on a trout stream in New Zealand after a long flight for him, and a much longer freighter ship ride for Katy and me.

So it seemed quite sudden—after all that traveling—for Junker and me to be up to our thighs in a New Zealand trout stream staring at two enormous trout feeding along the lip of a drop-off. I'd spotted the trout first, a fact that seemed to rile my friend. Katy was up in the hills somewhere hiking around that foreign country, scattering sheep and taking pictures of them.

"Now," I said, with a single nymph tied to a normal leader. "What do I do?"

"I don't know," Junker said, like he does. That is, all one word: *Iduhno*. And then he shrugged. "Cast at the fish, man."

Unsteadied by his casualness, I fired what I thought was a perfect cast at the fish on the left, which immediately spooked into the fish on the right, and just like that, the pool was empty.

"I can't believe you saw those trout before me," Junker said, like he was angry about it.

Then, his turn, he caught a trout from a backwater. And, later, after I spooked three more trout, he caught another. They were both big trout, with huge fins, humped greenish backs. They were magazine-quality brown trout. Katy took pictures of Kyle's trout, which seemed to highlight my ineptitude.

That was only day one: the start of what would be a multi-day slump.

"What am I doing wrong?" I asked.

"Iduhno," Junker shrugged.

⌒

Of course, Junker was demonstrating how to catch a fish in New Zealand every time he, well, caught a fish in New Zealand. Originally, I mistook his slow approach as part of his careful, slow-moving nature, and not a learned technique. Being the quintessential hustle player, I doubled down on my effort in lieu of my study, casting right between the eyes of every trout I saw, wondering if anyone had ever been skunked for an entire New Zealand summer in front of their new wife. Which made me think of the Thomas McGuane story where the wife of a permit fisher keeps saying *bear down* and the husband roars back *I am bearing down*. Was that our fate? Katy advising me to *bear down* while I unsuccessfully fired casts at big trout?

I eventually caught a New Zealand trout doing it my way, which meant it ate a fly that I rammed right between its eyes. I don't remember the trout at all. You'd think, after all that *bearing down* I'd have perfect recall of my first New Zealand trout, but I don't. But I guess, in the scope of what happened next, it makes sense. I knew as well as Junker that the fish was a fluke, the result of stubbornness.

Once I began paying attention to the fish, I got a whole lot better at catching them. If I understood what the fish were doing, I could usually fit myself—an entire person disguised as a fly—into their fate. I realized that fly-fishing is a series of miniature exercises of technique and thought bent toward a single deception. Map study. Gear check. Reorganize fly box. Well-tied fly. Tight knot. Observe the trout. Good cast. Fine drift. The cast to a feeding trout becomes the peak of a story the angler has been writing for at least months, if not years.

I'm not saying that I do this on every trout I see rise, or even on any given week, because I don't. Not even close. Not hardly ever. But it exists as an ideal, and when I find it, I find the steadiness that I often lack. This ideal is simple: I fish as if the upstream bull watches and I will find no other trout but *this* one, the one I see now. There is nothing beyond this trout, and behind this trout are only the steps that brought me to it.

Back to Michigan, pre-New Zealand: I once caught a three-inch trout that was rising in an impossible-seeming lie on the upper Manistee during a long upstream wade with Junker. We caught a lot of trout that day, and some nice ones. But in recounting the day over some sandwiches at Subway, Junker reminded me of the three-inch trout in front of the

stick, which seemed, to him, to stand above the rest as especially noteworthy. This wasn't something that made sense to
me then. But later I would see that it was connected to New
Zealand, or at least what New Zealand teaches an American angler about treating trout as a quarry as opposed to a
trophy. This was a lesson that Terry had learned long ago, as
evidenced by his final fascination with the small fish in front
of the lodge, and the ritual he'd devised—the series of individual movements and procedures—to catch some of them.

⌒

All of this explains, I think, why I value an afternoon of dry
fly-fishing like I had with Tank Ron on the Au Sable more
than I would, say, an equally productive day of streamer fishing. When a difficult day of fishing requires my best state of
being in order to catch a trout, then fishing becomes more
than fishing.

A half-mile past that first fish, Tanker and I found a line
of three trout rising along a high bank. They were all difficult
trout, all feeding in the slow water along a fast seam, along a
high bank protected by alders. The moodiness of the trout—
they were simply ignoring the duns—necessitated slowness.
Make a cast. Wait. Wait. Rise. Wait. Cast. If one of us botched

a cast, we had to wait even longer. But we succeeded in landing all three though it took an hour, and a lot of careful study, for the success to be complete.

The trout were big, fat Au Sable June brown trout. They were snooty, which in itself was a reward for two anglers who had dedicated a portion of their lives to combating snooty trout. Once hooked, the trout ran the line deep into the big river where it bowed against the slow but persistent current as the trout shot through the column to leap as brown trout leap in June, when they are in their prime. Fighting a trout provides tactile proof of their electricity. The author Jerry Dennis's wife, in his book *A Place on the Water*, described the tug of a fish as the hand of the earth.

I just love that.

I did whiff on one huge fish—clearly the biggest trout we'd seen so far. It was feeding in front of a logjam in relatively swift water. The rise form wasn't huge, but when it fed, its head created an enormous bulge in the surface, as if the surface were blown glass. It was, oddly, the easiest trout we'd found. It rose to my fly both times it saw it. But I didn't hook it on either rise. The first time, I thought I set the hook too quickly (as they say in New Zealand, *God Save the Queen* . . . and then set the hook) and then the second time, Tanker thought I set the hook too slowly. We argued about it briefly. Tanker told me exactly what I did wrong as if he were belittling one of his tank-trotting subordinates. I figured it was a big male with a kype so severe, the size 10 hook shot through the gap like a jet turning sideways to fit through a canyon: a scene from some Hollywood movie. In other words, as I told Tanker, *not my fault.*

"Yeah, whatever," he said.

A few other boats floated past and the clouds came in low and fast, but the wind went still. The clouds socked in and the evening turned dreary and the water temperature, never that warm, began to chill, slowing the hatch of brown drakes from a trickle to a drip. Then, the trout began roaming to find their food. They roamed the river with a graceful free-ranging impossibility. Now they were eating the duns.

This is how we found the biggest trout, the one that led us far upriver. It rose next to the boat, and, as we waited for it to rise again, it rose much farther upriver. Both rises were identical: the big head, the tail chasing the dorsal fin in a trout-spotted curve. I poled up to the scene of the last rise, only to realize, when the trout rose again, that we were fifty feet too short. The next rise, we were a hundred feet too short.

Okay, okay—we got this. I poled past *that* rise and kept going, racing to get within casting distance of the next rise *before the rise happened* and Tanker, upstream of me in the front of the boat, had his line trailing and his fly pinched in his fingers just waiting for a shot. But I couldn't close the gap and the trout rose again, sixty feet in front of us and going away and I began to wonder if the strategy of the trout to stay alive was superior to our strategy to catch it.

It was in this manner of racing against the next upstream rise that we shot past our friends' boat with Tanker yelling out when that big fish breached. I leaned back into the pole—if the pole had slipped on clay I would have fallen out of the boat—and tried to jump our boat ahead of the fish. The trout rose one last time at the head of the straightaway and then, around the upstream bend, we never saw it again. We held there waiting but it was gone. No drakes. Perhaps, if I'd looked, I would have discerned the faint outline of a bull on the bank, bellowing and stomping the swamp-ground. Because we held there, waiting. Waiting even as night fell, because at some point an upstream-feeding trout must turn around. Mustn't it? Then I said to Tanker *I guess that's it* and he cracked another beer and said *yuh-ep* like he does.

I turned around, angry about the trout. After all those big trout we'd caught, I was pissed about the one we hadn't, the proverbial one, the one that not only got away, but left us somewhere between joy and loss, and nothing but a few beers for our consoling. A trout like that . . . I couldn't think of a way to catch it. It seemed to be the most valuable trout I'd ever pursued. I stewed on it the rest of the evening and I'm still stewing on it.

It would be an old fish. Very old. They say a seven-year-old fish is old but I know it's not. There are trout that have been caught for five consecutive years, big browns that haven't grown an inch in that time, that still measure over twenty-four inches long—which, by growth rates, would make that fish much older than common knowledge dictates. After all, that big trout had to *grow* to that size first, which would take years. My friend Big Fish Johnny matches up the spot patterns on those big browns he hunts down, shows me pictures. He stares at me with such intensity I'm grateful not to have a reason to disagree with his convictions. I also know that biologists—in using scale samples to age the trout—have a hell of a tough time scraping scales from the biggest trout, and some they *can't* scrape any scales off of at all. Perhaps some of these trout are over a decade old, and through numerous captures and close calls, have devised strategies to avoid us pursuers . . . such as putting hundreds of feet between their rises.

One night—years ago—Tanker and I were sitting on the South Branch in a very secret spot. It was a windy dark evening and there was a cloud of gray drake spinners above us. There were a few good fish rising but none of them were rising consistently.

And then the biggest trout I've ever seen in the Au Sable rose across the river from us.

It rose going downstream.

It fed down the pool and down into the straightaway with big slow-motion head-to-tail rises. We could see the whole fish, the width of its head as great—or even greater—than that trout from the New Zealand meadow. *Butthole as big as a quarter*, is how Big Fish Johnny describes such trout.

I went running through the puckerbrush to get ahead of it, and I ended up kneeling on one knee next to a beaver run. The beavers have these muddy runs to the river and they provide dim little trails through the alders. The trout rose right in front of me. I flicked the fly into the river, just above the last rise. I thought, just maybe, this was the sort of trout I didn't want to hook. I felt like I had a galaxy worth of stars inside of me.

We never saw that trout again. Not that summer. Not ever.

Such memories revive the ghosts of trout past. It is too late to call a friend to talk through it. The guides are probably still out fishing so I can't call them either. I will just have these two trout in my head the rest of the night. My obsessiveness has little to do with dust or germs. I obsess about fish. I think trout occupy the loftiest pinnacle of aquatic guile, imbuing their waters with a magic that has seduced me from another life. I wonder if it is trout, and not the wolf or the New Zealand bull, which I should fear. My pursuit of trout has actually been consumption by trout: a freckled ideal, the best of which remain, too often, annoyingly unattainable.

CHAPTER 5: HEXING IN THE FERMATA

"The nice thing about putting on your glasses in the dark
is that you know you could see better if it were light, but
since it is dark the glasses make no difference at all."

—NICHOLSON BAKER, *A Box of Matches*

In the controversial Nicholson Baker novel *The Fermata,* Arno
Strine can stop time; a state of being he calls variously the
Fold, the Cleft, or the Fermata. In the Fermata, Arno can
walk autonomously among the frozen people. It's a superpower
that he uses voyeuristically (or worse). Arno's superpower is
diametrically opposite of what happens to me during the hex
hatch and the fermata it commands. I get stuck in the hex fermata for two weeks every year. I generally emerge unscathed,
though there is the niggling feeling—common to alien abduc-
tions and dreams—that something odd has been done to me.

When you're trapped in the hex fermata, you don't see your-
self, or the people around you, as frozen. After all, you are stuck
in the same place as all the other hex anglers: kicking trailer

tires in the fly shop parking lot, snooping out flies, telling stories with vicious hook sets and loud mouth-sounds meant to imitate a trout rising to the hex. There's Willy in the field trying to cast 175 feet. The guides are marching around like movie stars. The shop phone is ringing and I barely hear it, even though it's in my pocket. Caddis flutter throughout the gravel parking lot. I have two children, I remember, somewhere, somewhere distant, fluttering about like those caddis. . . .

Perhaps frozen is the wrong word. Or it needs an accompanying word. Glued: you are glued to the promise of the hex, and that holds you frozen in a figurative sense. For example, if the hex went on all year, I probably wouldn't be married with two kids. It never would have occurred to me that in being free to do what I want, and wanting one thing so badly, I wasn't free at all.

⌇

During hex, I openly disdain Mother Earth's hesitancy to turn her back to the sun. Like, when will it be dark so the fun can begin? During hex, the only time I feel awake *is* after dark. The daytime is a syrupy, humid impotency. The sweat beads on my neck like the ticking of seconds. Before we close the shop, we double and triple-check the car spots and the late hotel check-ins. At some point during the hex season we will miss one or the other, or both, and no one can really explain how that happens and no one is happy about it.

After work, at home, I take a power nap, known locally as *Daddy's Moment of Zen*, before a game of baseball with the kids. Around 9:00 p.m. I have a cup of coffee, throw two cold beers in the cooler, hop in the fish truck, and make a dust cloud. By 10:15 p.m. I know I'll hear hex wings in the air. By midnight I'll be locked into the bass-drum rise of a big trout. There are no global considerations when you're in the hex fermata. It's not pure living. It's not particularly good living. But treated as a two-week one-off, it's fun.

⌇

As I'm already wading through the hex fermata, I have to remember the first night my dad and I fished the hex. This was *really* long ago, the day before my very first day working at the Gates Lodge fly shop. Dad and I stopped into the fly shop for a consultation with Rusty, unaware at the time that *everyone* stopped in for a consultation with Rusty, and he put a few hex flies in a box for us and told us to go fish the South Branch. Where? Wherever there wasn't already a fish-truck parked.

We ended up at an old stone wall bordering a fast riffle. We went out into the middle of the riffle and just stood there. Downriver we could see two guys sitting on a bank. They were both staring at us. *This doesn't feel right*, my dad said. I remember that. We ended up sitting on the bank in some flatter water upriver. At dark, the trout began rising in the darkness, and I cast at them for a half-hour. My memory has certainly been warped—not by time, but by the subsequent years of hex fishing. The river was dark, but it seemed there was an even *darker* corner, and in that corner the big trout were rising, exploding in a scattershot of munitions carrying various levels of charge. A strange whirring roar came from the sky: a noise that emanated, I would later learn, from nighthawks dive-bombing on the swarming spinners.

This wasn't like any trout water I'd ever fished. A trout river at night is not the same trout river during the day, especially if it is a brown trout river. My fate seemed unattached to my waving of a fly rod or one of Rusty's flies. It was a communication problem between the trout and me. The trout were rising all around me, but I didn't know how to catch them. When the trout quit rising, I was glad to escape back to regular life.

The next night, I joined a kid who also worked at the shop—Alex—for some more night fishing. It went just like the night before: I think I spent the whole night casting at a bouncing stick. Alex didn't catch anything either. We were just kids then, getting sucked up the portal. Starting that night, we went fishing every night together—and I mean, every night—bouncing around the dirt roads in Alex's maroon Dodge Caravan with the fake wood panels. We fished everywhere. All the time. He was staying at one of Rusty's friend's cabins for the summer, and we would tie flies at the picnic table outside, the South Branch sliding by red and dark in the valley below. We smashed our hair stackers into that picnic table, a pile of hex imitations accumulating in the cigar boxes in front of us, talking excitedly about our plan for that night, the promise of those hex. . . . We were just rich as kings on it.

∽

During hex, expectations are as outsized as the bugs and the trout. It's a trout fisher's harvest season—the end of the hex is like the first frost to the gardener. Though a fly fisher's frost—that time after hex—is really wonderful. It's just hard to see it as such when there's a size 6 mayfly hatching every night and big browns rising to them.

The hex is a giant, nocturnal mayfly that, in habit, has as much in common with a locust as it does other mayflies. By the Great Lakes, they hatch in biblical profusion, swarming streetlights, accumulating like snow on bridges. Their spinner flights create an electrical tension in the air, and the morning after a mating flight the river stinks of rot. It is a hatch without nuance. It is the most predictable mayfly, in my opinion, and because of this predictability, size, quantity, and nocturnal-ness, big brown trout love them. *Love them.* I think the hex is so tantalizing to an adult brown trout that the same fish is caught two or more times in the same evening by the ever-increasing train of drift boats that now float the river.

Skipping a night during the hex hatch produces in me a sulking despondency that seems the denial of an addictive chemical. Which I'm sure on some level it is. Part of this is just my love for trout fishing. The other part of this is working in a fly shop. Not a lot of people know this, but working in a fly shop breeds in the worker the desire to go fishing. I think we just get revved up talking about it. In the morning, I'll vow to take a night off from fishing, and by 2:00 p.m. I've got three competing game plans as to where I'll fish that evening (and a few backup plans for each game plan).

My fishing journal, so painstakingly kept all winter and spring, *nearly* skips the time between June 21 (an innocent entry about a mink capturing a fish) and July 1—a clear indication that I'd been frozen for some time, except for one surviving journal entry when I emerged from the fermata long enough to at least take a stab at keeping it up.

July 1

Just after midnight, I was crouched on a slightly raised bank on the South Branch with my headlamp off. There was a large fish rising in the river just below me. I couldn't see the rise, of course, but it sounded like the rise of a good fish. Out in the middle of the purple river I could make out the faint outline of the angler who was casting at the fish. Every so often, the angler would whistle appreciatively when the trout produced an especially strong rise. Normally I'd have snuck off to find another fish, but I'd been trying to find a fish all evening that didn't already have someone casting at it. I wasn't but fifteen feet from the trout, on a small bluff above it. The whistling angler's hex also whistled as it was whipped back and forth to dry it. This is a rhythm particular to hex fishing. *Whip, whip, cast. Whip, whip, cast.* Many hex anglers don't fish anything else *but* hex. They do what they were taught: *whip, whip, cast.* But some of these old hex anglers are still pretty good at what they do. The whistler hooked the trout from that tough back-water spot (though the rise, a big splashy rise, told me the trout ate the fly as it dragged across its nose), and as the trout churned the water I stood quietly and walked off, cloaked by the thrashing of the fish and the loud sound of a click reel.

I walked down to the big cedar swamp. There was a flash-light coming through the cedar swamp, so I shut off my red light and crouched on one knee and averted my eyes so they didn't reflect in the angler's light. He walked by me no more than four yards away. One or both of his wader legs had leaked and he was really slogging through the woods and wheezing with the weight of the water. As soon as he was by, I snuck down the same trail he'd used to exit the water, turning on my red light, hoping he'd see it, so it seemed I'd appeared from nowhere. I entered the cedar swamp, which isn't really a swamp, just a grove of mature cedars standing over a bed of roots and moss.

As I approached the river, another red light flashed in my direction: a gentle warning, the night fisher's low growl. I turned off my light and crouched next to a cedar, separated from the angler by a veil of tag alders. I could hear a few different trout feeding: a gulper, and a smasher. Just like in New Zealand, the trout have different frequencies. The angler was casting upstream to them. I knew there was a big muck bank behind a logjam and that probably the trout were there, rising next to the bank. He called out to me, once, I thought . . . but I didn't really hear what he said. His headlamp was low on batteries and was bleating a soft red light warning him of this fact. Then he began whispering to the fish. I knew who he was, I realized. *C'mon*, he said.

A sound behind me . . . and a light. It was the water-slosher returning.

A holler: Carl—you still have fish working?

And Carl, the man in the river, said, *a few!*

The slosher: I'm soaked, I'll be in the truck.

Carl, impatient: *Alright.*

I was stuck between them, with the slosher on the far side of the cedar swamp and Carl right next to me and Carl saying, *okay, okay, goddammit,* quietly as the slosher sloshed off. Another light beamed from an angler below us, and Carl flashed the red light downstream to fend him off. *Goddammit,* he said again. Then two more lights appeared upstream and Carl had to fend them off also with his increasingly dim red light. Meanwhile the trout he was casting at were rising frantically, sending inviting splashes and gulps up and down the river, attracting anglers from throughout the dark wood. Those rising trout were like uncovered food to a bunch of houseflies. We were all gathered around Carl and his two trout.

A particularly loud splash: the zip of line drawing tight. *Shit!* The fly came free or broke off . . . a snap on the frustrated re-cast. Break-off. The worst. The worst way to lose a big fish.

Goddammit.

Goddammit, I whispered.

I waited until he moved in the water to move myself. When I moved, Carl stopped, having heard me. *Hello?* He called, but I was feeling my way through the cedar swamp and then, after a face full of cedar bough, I flicked on my red light and kept walking and heard the loud sound behind me of Carl leaving the river. It is impossible, I thought, to leave a river quietly.

By the time his light crossed the main trail I was far down

the path, huffing and puffing, clomping along like fly fishers do at night. A single light approached along the trail and we shared a quick late-night acknowledgment, both of us walking quickly past each other.

My plan was to slide into the bottom of the horseshoe and see if I could find a few fish still feeding on the duns. After a whole night of not fishing, and my morning alarm due to explode in less than five hours, I was ready to find a trout or two for myself.

I came to a bend, but it put me between two anglers. The lower angler was on the bend downstream and casting to a fish that sounded pretty tricky and was probably on the wrong side of a log parallel to the current. I could see the log in the silver river projecting upstream from a fist-shaped logjam like a middle finger, and the trout was rising on my side— the bank side—of the middle finger. At least that's what it seemed to me. The casting angler had luminescent fly line and threw tight loops, and if the fish were on the angler's side he would have caught it. Then, well, he caught it. So maybe I just don't know anything. It sounded like a massive trout when it rose, but the angler fought it smartly and cautiously. Some hex anglers hook trout and then pull as hard as they can, bringing the trout to the surface, where it flips around and jumps and often throws the fly. Better to play them firmly but gently, and keep them in the water until the net slides under them. Done correctly, it's like the trout submits to a gentle release and, after a brief respite, a return to feeding on yet more hex.

The other angler was far upstream, existing only as the flash of light on the far bank. It seemed he was scanning for bugs, which meant he probably hadn't found a fish yet, and was contemplating whether there was enough bugs to interest a trout . . . or if he should leave, or try something else.

I'd had that experience a few nights earlier. The hex hadn't hatched, and so I'd fished a big wet fly upstream in the slack water and had caught two dandy trout hand-twisting the fly back to me. It was a foggy evening and the river was quiet. No anglers and no forest sounds, just the fog and a yellow half moon. The trout ate so hard—the pull was so spellbinding— that I fished a foot at a time up the soft side of a long riffle hoping for a few more of those pulls and the time just went away from me. I just let my mind go wherever it wanted, and I cast up into the slack water and did the hand twist, which provided a natural cadence to my thoughts. I thought about all the great times I'd had in and around that riffle, since a much-younger me was resting on an elbow lobbing pebbles into the big stillwater upstream and a much-younger Junker was casting at the rings from the pebbles thinking it was a grand trout. When he stopped to change his fly, I lobbed another pebble. *Well son of a . . . !* That stretch of the South Branch is very special to me and these beautiful things always seem to happen to me when I fish it.

The upstream light went off, and I was glad. If his light had stayed on, it would have meant he didn't see any hex and was soon to leave. But the light off . . . that meant he'd seen some bugs, and now was going to sit in the dark and listen for a fish.

This left a nice run for me to fish between the successful luminescent angler downstream and the upstream light shiner, a hundred-yard cobble-bottomed riffle with a long muck bank down one side and a row of cedar sweepers down the other side. In the dark, the river appeared simultaneously narrower and wider than normal: if I looked to the cedars, it seemed a small stream; if l looked toward the muck bank and the row of alders along it, it seemed silver and vast and still. I slipped in at the head of the bend and began to sneak through the still side of the river, thinking I'd find a hex fish rising along the muck side. Thinking: *light off, ears on.*

I'd anticipated a rise on the muck-side, but the three trout I ended up finding were rising on the shallow-side between the sweepers. The moon had burst through the clouds, immediately flooding the dark river with stage light, and that's when those trout started rising in the cedar shadows.

I crossed the river and waded up behind the sounds of their rising until I could see them feeding in the night glare. Two of the trout were rising on a seam coming off the tip of a log and their rises were exuberant and easy to see in the moonlight. The other trout was somewhere in the shadows behind the jam, and the only way I could see the rise was to put my head down to the water and wait—a few seconds after the rise came I'd see some waves distort the reflection of the moon. That trout was way back there and sounded huge.

I caught the first two, the second proving more difficult than the first. They were nice trout. Healthy. Fat. Young. Nothing special. That last trout took a half hour of dapping. I'd get the fly about three feet from my tip-top, and, like a fencer, I'd stab the rod tip into the darkness and hope my fly was actually on the water. When the trout rose, I'd set the hook, and then untangle the fly from the cedar above me. This went on so long it began to become the point of the evening. Then the trout ate in a great echoing rise, and I pulled it from the jam, thrashing, and I let it swim around for a moment to calm both it and myself. I'd thought it would be huge, but it was the same as the others: a healthy two-pound trout, clean and fresh in June. The echoes of its rise had been merely that, echoes.

I left the river and walked back to my vehicle.

I kept the waders on, and started driving east.

⁓

Too much of trout fishing is about the conquest, and too much of this journal has been about conquest. A conquest seems to illustrate success against previously insurmountable odds and this sort of thing *is* tempting to write about. For instance, the reader may have guessed what I'm to write next: that, after sneaking away from the South Branch, I headed downriver to a crowded boat ramp, waded up the weed edge at 3:00 a.m., spied a big trout rising in the moonlight, and caught it to the surprise of a drift boat full of very drunk light-shiners who didn't know I was there. The reader might further guess that I snuck back to the parking lot unseen, *stole* a beer from someone's cooler that had been left unattended, and then drove down the dirt road drinking said beer, lawless and autonomous, and reeking of lemon-eucalyptus bug spray, before crashing into bed for what would be two hours of sleep before spending a day milling around the front of the fly shop shaking hands and telling stories and seeing how far Willy was casting, which was pretty damn far, and visiting Dennis behind Room 3 while he smoked a menthol and told one of his perfect stories about the night he and Matt had, before I returned to the shop to double-check car spots and late check-ins to the hotel before I headed home to grab a nap, play some baseball, and then brewed the cup of coffee that would propel me back into the night, and the beginning of yet another week of lost journal entries and odd, dreamy memories.

Maybe I did.

Or maybe I drove to the popular landing, and—while balanced on a logjam attempting to dap at a rising fish—fell from my perch and into the water, providing splashing, spotlight-lit entertainment for two or three drift-boats that were rowing to the landing. Of course, being a fly shop owner, I had to submerge and hold onto an underwater piece of debris, much like a shot duck, so as not to have the story blasted on social media. Then I had to crawl out of the river through twenty feet of muck, undress there in the long grass, empty the water from my waders, and walk back to the parking lot in my long johns, while listening to tales of my failure both to balance on the logjam *and* to conceal my identify shared loudly among the semi-drunk hex anglers, their eyes shining red in the fermata, as I slipped quietly into my truck.

Maybe that happened instead.

～

In *The Fermata*, Arno has something close to complete autonomy. He could freeze the world and walk through it doing as he pleased, and it's too bad Arno wasn't a trout fisher, because maybe, with supernatural adjustment, he could have frozen all those anglers in place but kept the trout streams flowing. That would be nice. That would be a nice thing to do. That sort of autonomy within the fermata: I've felt it once or twice. But one old guide, who my friend called Wheels . . . well, I think Wheels felt it all the time.

Here's the impossible thing Wheels could do: he could weave an Au Sable riverboat through a river of boats at midnight without a flashlight, which, honestly, is like doing the slalom down a mountain with your eyes closed. Late at night, he would do circles in the weed beds with his riverboat, flushing the accumulated hex spinners from the stalks and into the main river, where he would pick off the trout that began rising to this unexpected chum line. On those odd nights when the river was coated in bug and nary a rise, he would throw rocks into the river to imitate a trout rise, and people I know, his clients, insist that this worked. He had a secret riverboat move that he used to approach quiet trout sipping along the bank. It's now my preferred method for hex fishing.

When I floated a stretch I knew he was floating, I would listen in the dark to see if I could find him. He'd be in front of me. Then, somehow, he was behind me. How close had we passed? How blind was I? Occasionally his location would be marked by the sound of a trout thrashing in the night. He only assumed human form in the headlights at the boat ramp: a cheery, barrel-chested man, with a quirky, kept-secret smile.

Once a few buddies and I needed help processing a deer, and so we took it to Wheels's house. He'd mentored one of my friends, as he'd mentored many other youths. I was starstruck. He and his wife led us through the process in their basement room. The room was specifically designed for cleaning deer. We used fillet knives for working off the silverskin, and put the meat in plastic bowls, which his wife either set aside or fed through the very old, electric meat grinder. They told me they used to can venison and send it to their kids when their kids were in college.

A few days after the deer processing, I ran into him at the Grayling Township Hall on Election Day. Seeing him, I froze just when the kind lady asked for my precinct. She had to repeat the question.

Mike smiled at me.

"What, you need me to show you how to vote, too?" He said to me.

Man.

A few years later his kids wanted to book him a float and they came to the lodge where, many years ago, he'd guided for Cal Gates. Wheels had recently and quite quickly developed dementia. His daughter told me that they'd taken him bluegill fishing on a lake, and after an hour of bluegill fishing he'd stood up in the boat and just stepped over the gunnel and into the lake. This seemed impossible to me. I think, repeatedly, that some people are immortal . . . so good are they at life.

Our guides were booked on the date they wanted, so I volunteered to take him for a free float. A week later, I picked him up at his house. He was just standing in his yard.

"Wanna go fishing?" I said through my window.

He held a feather to me, a primary feather from a crow, I thought. "Here's a feather," he said.

We loaded up his stuff, drove to the river. A bunch of locals were down at the launch and they all knew him and glared at me somewhat accusingly as I shoved their native boat off the trailer. What was *I* doing with *him*? That question seemed appropriate. And one I couldn't really answer.

Wheels knew the locals but he couldn't remember them, like a taste the mind can't place. One local guide—his name was Lacey—was talking to him, and kept saying his own name clearly, *Lacey*, and Wheels kept saying *Who*? And he kept doing it, until I was about to tell Lacey to knock it off. And then Wheels started laughing like he was faking and then Lacey laughed too like it was the best joke he'd ever heard and maybe it was.

It seemed to me that his mind had lost the connection between his memories and his mouth. He had all these stories that would come to him as we floated and then they'd just evaporate. *Right here was the . . . it's called . . .* He threw tight loops at the bank with a dry skunk—a local rubber-legged fly—on our short float together. He didn't hide his disappointment that we were quitting before dark and made fun of the size of the fish he was catching. He didn't seem particularly excited to be fishing with *me*, but then it was difficult to tell. Mostly he just twitched the skunk. He could really twitch a skunk well.

Over the years, I suppose, I'd watched Wheels's edge—his masterful autonomy—dull. One lodge guest who is as close to

Wheels, fishing-wise, as a kid's stuffed cat toy is to a cheetah, criticized his ability to back-up a trailer. Another time, while wade fishing, I saw him crash his riverboat into a log structure. I heard rumor that he wasn't guiding much anymore. His wife passed away. He'd hung up his skis. Once, when in the fly shop lamenting the catch-and-release regulations, he quite clearly lost what he was saying, despite it being a point that he was passionate about, and waved at me before leaving the shop basically in mid-sentence.

Coincidentally, Terry and Wheels were neighbors, and they both wore thick glasses and were, as I review my knowledge of both of them, remarkably similar. Terry was a swimmer and a trout angler and Wheels was a skier and a trout angler. Both taught science: Wheels high school biology, Terry college chemistry. They were so diametrically opposed in aesthetic and opinion, however, that they became somewhat similar in that way in which very opposite things can be similar, like trout and nighthawks are very similar, if only for their shared love of swooping in on hex spinners. And both Terry and Wheels were free of the hex fermata. Terry because he fished hex like they were any other hatch, and, similarly, Wheels because the hex was just another season, like deer hunting or duck hunting or skiing, and I don't believe it drew more reverence from him than any other outdoor sport. He'd just done it his whole life. And was taught by others who had done it *their* whole lives. And on back, back through the timber days and the grayling, back when Grayling was named Milltown and the streets were packed sand.

When he was in his prime, the few times I saw Wheels on the river, he'd always be doing something different than I normally did it. He'd be holed up in a side channel I'd never consider holing up in. He'd be sucked up tight to a grassy bank on what I thought was the wrong side of the river.

Once, when I was cooking my sports' dinner on the clay bluff below the North Branch, he came paddling down the river, an ancient client slumped in the bow. Wheels, with his full-brim hat pulled tight against the sun, his beavertail paddle working much harder than normal, directed the river-boat right at a logjam and then dug the paddle, avoiding the obstruction by inches, rousing his ancient client from his nap, and drawing, for a second, a secret smile from the man in the back of the boat toward *me*. I'd just started guiding then, and that smile seemed an acknowledgment of professional similarity.

⁓

But, like I said, the edge had dulled. By the time I floated Wheels, he had a few full sentences for me but not much else. All I had to offer him was a float down the river and when it was done, it was done, and I didn't know what to think. Driving home, he stared out the passenger window, a light smile on his face, and I wondered if he even knew who I was. I'd wanted to convey that in a roundabout way I'd learned a lot from him, a quiet float of thanks. But that's not what it was, really. Nope, it seemed to me I'd just wanted to be near the secret for a day. Much like I want to be in the river at night, when the big secrets swim through the fermata. No, I didn't think he knew who I was. Or maybe he did. Maybe it was easy for him to know who I was without even remembering my name. Maybe it was pretty simple to Wheels: I was an out-of-towner who released his keeper-sized trout and still used a flashlight at night.

To him, I was just another of the frozen ones.

CHAPTER 6: NORTHERN LIGHTS: A JOURNAL

He's like a perfect, windless pond . . . You throw
something in just to watch it sink, and you're
going to see it on the bottom staring back
at you for the rest of your life.

—LAUREN GROFF, *Florida*

July 6

There comes a time during hex season when the addictiveness
of the big mayflies and big trout fades just enough for my real
life to resume. Maybe it's burnout from all the late nights,
or my big-trout appetite is sated, or maybe it's both of these
things. But before my hex season is truly over, Holden joins
me for a father-son float. This has become an annual tradition.
He's just finished his school year and can stay up late. I've just
finished our busiest season at the lodge and want to spend
time with my family. Tonight we are on the Manistee, a river
that begins, like the Au Sable, near the city of Gaylord; but

whereas the Au Sable heads east into Lake Huron, the Manistee turns west and flows into Lake Michigan.

As I unload the canoe, Holden stands by the river, shrinking into his oversized Cabela's boot-foot waders, fidgeting with mosquitoes. I think fly-fishing must be the best thing for a kid, with its mix of action and adventure. Still, it has to be the right kind of adventure. It can't be the kind of adventure I usually have, in which the adventure occurs on the way to or from the actual fly-fishing in the form of a stuck truck or getting lost. No, the adventure has to be a *part of* the fly-fishing.

This takes a bit of luck.

We launch the canoe and I pole the craft upstream. This is a special stretch of river, clear water flowing over old logs scattered in tan sand and beds of bright green watercress. I pass the Money Hole, and the big flat where my friend Matt Verlac, a fishing guide up here, had a fish of a lifetime spend about thirty feet of a streamer retrieve examining the fly, and past the big bend I call the Grandpa Pool, and through the islands, and finally to the tail-out of the run I call the Promised Land. And then I start cussing. I cuss for a good minute and Holden lets me.

"What?"

"I forgot the fly rods."

I tell him about Terry and the forgotten bait and he listens and slaps at mosquitoes.

"So are we just going to go home?"

"No," I say. But I know already this has become the wrong type of adventure.

We float downstream silently, back to the beginning. I get the rods from the top of the vehicle, where I left them, and return to the canoe.

"It's better to just go do it right," I say, leaning into the boat pole, propelling us upstream. "I was so mad. And now I'm happy again. It's like it never happened."

"I guess," he says, and yawns.

I pole up to the main river and through the S-bends. There are many good pools in this stretch of river. Some of the pools are good all the time for all the hatches. Others are only good during the hex. Some are good for the hatching hex. Some are good for the spinners. I love this water and feel I know it well. I don't know it as well as some other people know it, but I know which pools are which.

The Promised Land is a long right bend with a bank of leaning cedars. The river not only cuts into the cedars, it trick-
les behind the cedars, and pushes deep, deep beneath them
opulently. There's a small seam that bifurcates the deep water
beneath the cedars. I'd been at the tail of the Promised Land
when I'd realized I'd forgotten the fly rods. Now the pool,
even with the cedar bank and the sweet seam and the dark
memories of trout thrashing whitely in the black water, seems
cursed.

I think of the kid already eating Chex Mix, and how, last
year and the year before, he fell asleep in the boat just when
the fishing got good.

I turn the boat around.

"What did you forget this time?"

"I forgot that last year you fell asleep. And the year before
you fell asleep too. So it wouldn't make much sense to go all
the way back up there only to have you fall asleep again. Last
year I caught all the big trout while you were sleeping."

"I was seven last year."

I spend a moment remembering when every birthday magi-
cally seemed to catapult me up one tier in strength and overall
capability. And in some ways, it did. One birthday a kid is just
a kid. The next birthday he can drive 75 miles per hour on the
super slab.

∽

I decide to park us on the Money Hole, an unimaginative name often bestowed upon the last good pool in any float. You know, the one where the client catches the big fish in the ninth inning and, at the handshake, slips the guide a little extra. I think it's more guide shack legend than anything. But then again, the Money Hole *has* been an awfully good fishing spot over the years.

I plop the anchor on the sandbar. It's dusk already. The mosquitoes are terrible. I see a few hex spinners flying upstream. They are not flying up the main river. Instead, they are hanging a left and flying up the mucky side channel at the head of the pool. That side channel disappears into a lily pad seep deep in the forest. Those spinners, I think, either know exactly what they're doing, or don't have a clue. I've seen Hendrickson spinners clotting the dark, warm surface of the state highway instead of the South Branch, just a hundred yards away. I wonder if eventually the spinners that are attracted to roads will be selected, for obvious reasons, for evolutionary failure. This, I think, would be a good thing.

A few trout rise but the boy struggles to get his cast right. He's anxious for Chex again. I let him eat and crack the only beer I brought and force myself to chill. The busy season is over. The rest of the season—the one that seemed so unbear-

able while trapped within the hex fermata—will be as refresh-
ing as cold water after a couple months of summer toil. The
wimpy tricos, Terry's favorite hatch, will provide hours of fishing as whimsical as they are technical. The creeks beckon from
within their alder tunnels. The night fishing calls like a loon at
dusk. I know there's nothing to this skin-walker thing, but I
just can't shake the conviction that I've got something stalking
me now that hadn't been stalking me before. It's not exactly a
mid-life crisis. It's just my first clear view of the end of myself.
Or maybe that *is* a mid-life crisis. I tend to think a mid-life
crisis is a luxury. Maybe having a skin-walker is a luxury, too,
a sign of feeling you have something to lose. Overheard at a
swanky party: *Do you even have a skin-walker, bro?*

At dark, the hex begin hatching out of the muck channel—
the same muck channel the spinners flew up. I can see them
on the water, bouncing to dry their wings. They are black on
the silver glare, as if they have been stamped out of the metal
surface. I'm whispering to Holden as we hear the popping of
rising fish eating the emerging duns way up the muck flat,
explaining it to him. The trout are feeding in the lily pads
now, I whisper, but soon the uneaten duns will float down to
the main river and the trout will set up on the seam that flows
along the bushes.

And they do.

The water is too deep for Holden to wade so I move the
canoe into position. He uses my favorite hex rod, which is a

snappy modern fiberglass six-weight, strung with a glow-line, and nine feet of leader tapered to 2x. I have fished this rig all hex season and I know the rod and the leader. I know my box of flies and distances and drifts. The blink of the fireflies, the last frog songs of the summer, the mosquito hum, the rise of the trout have all become a language that I once knew, thought I forgot, and now, at the height of the season, feel the return of fluency.

I get out of the canoe and stand next to where he's seated in the bow. He's still eating Chex Mix—I bought him the big bag. I grab the big bag from his hands, crumple the contents into dust, and dump the dust into the river.

"Silence," I say.

He laughs. And, I think, he understands. The bugs are pouring from the river and the trout are gulping from the shadows. For a kid who loves to read classic African hunting books, this sort of big game showmanship makes sense. This, I think, is the right kind of adventure.

There are three big fish rising. By now, Holden can cast. His cast is not right, really. The thumb leaves the cork on the back cast. But he's been casting long enough that somehow he forces it to work. His mend, his line feed, speaks to his learning to fish on a river like the Au Sable. The boy fools, hooks, and loses all three trout. I think back to my first hex experience, and it doesn't seem fair that his half-distracted brain was able to hook all three trout. He's a native to his home water and I'm not. Perhaps he'll be a famous guide. Perhaps he'll design clothes. Either way, this is what he'll think of when he thinks of trout water.

"We'll come back tomorrow," I say. "We'll get these sons-of-bitches tomorrow," I tell him. Cussing, he understands, is something to be done on the river.

There is one more big fish rising and the kid hears it. "I'm done for tonight. You can try for him."

"You sure?"

"Yep."

"Okay. But I'm going to talk you through it."

I explain to him how I want to stop the rod high and to the right, then drop the rod tip with the line, perhaps shaking in some slack while it drops. The trout eats on the first cast. It's the first good night of hex up here and the trout are easy to fool on the big flies.

I hand Holden the rod. He fights it patiently, whispering to it. The trout is longer than his shoulders are wide, a nice male. The kid holds it across his lap. The moon is in the cedar tops. I take the picture and he asks to see it on the phone.

"Those are two things I love," I tell him.

He thinks about it. "Oh I get it," he says.

July 7

We bring the riverboat this time because it will pole upstream easier and is more stable. This time there'll be no heading upriver to the Promised Land. Holden has told me he wants another shot at those trout in the Money Hole. This time, he helps me load the boat and though his waders are still over-sized, he no longer appears to be shrinking into them. More importantly, at the corner store, I caught him squeezing various bags and snacks. I asked him what he was doing and he said he was *checking for quietness.*

The Raft Guy—a person I've met before and know only as the Raft Guy—is a bend or two above us. We hear him cough and I know it's him. It's cold—much colder than the night before. There are no rises at dusk. We see no spinners, and at dark I see no hatchers. But at full dark we begin to hear the big fish rising along the far bank. Holden hears them too with eager ears.

There are—I count them out, pointing—six good fish rising along the bank . . . more than the night before. Less bugs, more fish. Who knows? We mark them by gloomy landmark. There is bush fish, white birch fish #1, white birch fish #2, cedar fish, shadow fish, and, at the tail-out, what I suppose is the fish we caught last night. There is a soft trickle of hatching bugs.

In succession, and without fanfare, Holden hooks bush fish, cedar fish, back up for white birch fish #2, white birch fish #1, and then, at long last, shadow fish, and loses . . . them . . . all. All because, I think, he can't set the hook hard enough with the fiberglass rod. The fish are hooked, the rod strains, and then the fly comes back. Every time.

Late in the hatch a few fish began rising in the cedars where shadow fish was, and these new fish are big fish. I hook a *whopper*—a giant—that comes unhooked. Then I go up and hook what I think is white birch fish #2 back on the feed. I hand the rod to Holden and he fights it and lands it. *You deserve to hold that fish*, I say. *You fished beautifully tonight.*

Now, he wants to fish again, and I can see the hex wheels turning now, the dark river visible to him, Plato's cave and all that. Another fish is rising in the backwater shadows.

I park the boat.

"Little further down," Holden whispers. And I will forever cherish him commanding me to do this. It is everything about his subtle, precise nature . . . the one that I see when we are hunting squirrels and he's waiting for the squirrel—aloft in a mammoth oak tree—to lift its head the necessary millimeter more.

I scoot down a foot.

"Right here," he says.

I watch the glow line unfurl. I see him flip his perfect mend—the boy was born with a perfect mend. He shakes the rod tip to let out some slack. Repeat. Repeat. And then the trout eats his fly . . . and comes off. Again.

August 1

The chute is a fast, narrow band of water—maybe fifteen feet wide—with as many feet of dead water on either side of it. Above the chute is a wide, shallow riffle that is ankle-deep in the summer. Below the chute is a slow bend pool that spreads into a tail-out as shallow as the riffle above it.

We are here because I know he can wade it. When I fish with someone with limited mobility, I initially lament the lack of options. Invariably, this lamentation transforms into a delicious new challenge, and I find the fishing is great in spots I'd normally not consider going. Notably, earlier in the spring, Holden's height led to a wonderful evening on the North Branch. We caught a pile of trout rising to sulphurs in the many bubble lines of the big shallows upstream of the town of Lovells. Neither of us got our knees wet. Such limitations in his wading have led us to this easy spot on the South Branch to try some mouse fishing.

We wade into the fast water of the chute, my hand on his thin shoulder.

"They should be right up in this fast water with this heat," I whisper to Holden.

The river is too fast for a straight swing so I tell him to cast across the fast water and mend upstream and follow the line with the rod-tip. This should slow the swing down, allowing the fly to hang on the seams of the chute. Good cast, I tell him. Don't forget to mend. I have my finger hooked to the strap of his waders. It's a dark, sticky night filled with no-see-ums. Holden keeps asking me about the house on the hill with the lights. He wants to know who owns it, and if he's a nice guy, and if he hunts, and if he fishes, and why the dogs I said would bark at us aren't barking at us.

Betwixt these questions, the river opens up with a single resonating thrum.

"Got him," the boy says. "*Big one.*"

The glow-line stretches tight, from the throbbing slant upward from the river, through hooped fly rod, and into the luminescent reel buried in the boy's sternum. I've never felt *bolted* to a trout, but this boy is *bolted* to a trout. Through my finger hooked through his wader suspenders, I'm like a small appliance drawing from a much larger breaker.

Then the connection gives. The hook pulls. The boy, as if touching an alternating current electric fence, is thrown back into me. I turn on my headlamp and examine the foam bug and see the tooth marks across the back of it. Three tooth marks across a half inch of foam. Big trout. I see also the fly never moved. When the fish ate, it clamped so tight into the foam that the hook set never actually set the hook. The fish held long enough to cast a spell. It never splashed, ran, leapt. It held in the dark, as strong as the boy. And when it decided the taste of foam wasn't worth it, it expelled the fly, suddenly releasing the tension.

August 3

Went back for the fish in the chute last night. In the rain. In the hot rain. I thought this might be the night, and Holden thought so too. We fished slowly and every inch of the entire bend. We fished it with the Night Bean, a fly I tied specifically for Holden to fish because I thought the deer hair might allow the fly to slide through the fish's teeth (and the hook into the jaw).

The Night Bean did not work.

August 5, August 6, August 10

Three swings, three misses. School has begun for Holden— he's on a locally offered Extended Learning Year that's great for parents who must work nearly every day in the summer. Katy tells me that such late-night endeavors on school nights are leading to tiredness and tantrums. She thinks it's the lack of sleep, but I know it's the lack of fish.

We never move, hear, or see a fish in the chute. The big one has the run of the pool. It is the only needle in that haystack. And a big trout like that, it can be anywhere in the pool. *Anywhere.*

August 17

"Boy, I think we're done with that fish," I tell him. "The summer is too short and the world too big to keep fishing the same forty yards of water. Tonight, we're going to float."

He raises his hands in victory. Double-A, Holden's now six-year-old younger brother, looks at me. "When do I go?"

"Soon," I say. The thought of guiding Double-A in the river at night produces the same adrenaline dread of being locked in a dark room with a predatory animal. Though he does generate high line speeds in lawn casts, it is almost always when provocation—real or imagined—prompts him to launch a stinging attack at one of us. Also, he has almost never not fallen out of a boat. "Real soon. In the daylight."

It's a perfect dark-of-the-moon night. I drag a canoe through the woods to the river and Katy runs the car shuttle for us. Double-A is in the back seat and I make a big show of handing him a dollar for his having "helped" us move the vehicles. He stares at the buck, nods, and stares evenly at me. Deal.

Holden's casting with the big fly and heavy floating line has improved tremendously now. He uses two hands on the cork to whip the fly into a nice splat about thirty feet from the boat. The river is alive, the dark permeated by the odd pops and swirls of feeding trout. This is random activity. A moth. A frog. A mouse. A cream midge. Between spots, Holden shines the light. The beam uncovers those big browns from the dark. They dart and glide in the shallows, slide sideways along the lip of a drop-off.

"It's going to happen tonight," I tell him.

Below what I call the Cathedral, it does. The take is silent. The line draws tight. I turn on the light, leap from the canoe, drop the anchor, and run around the bow with the net. It's a fine brown trout, not quite eighteen inches. It's not the big one in the Chute. But the boy is excited.

We quit fishing and I paddle down to the launch. Holden is on his knees at the bow, using the light to steal the river from the dark. Those browns scatter silently back to the ink.

Later, he holds the light as I load up the canoe.

August 26

So I've got to write about what happened yesterday.

We—the whole family—headed to my favorite bass lake on a windy 75-degree day with cold hidden in the wind but not the air. We caught a few fish on drop-shot rigs. Really, though, the fishing was poor. The bass were not aggressive and the wind was from the east. Twice I caught fish while untangling the boys and my rubber worm was just sitting on the bottom. Holden was frustrated with the slow fishing. Double-A was frustrated that the lake water was too cold for a swim. I was frustrated because I'd hurt my back a few days earlier and the spasms were pulsing directly behind my diaphragm.

That evening, we decided to go fly-fishing downstream, below the Mio dam. Well, I decided. But they all came along.

The white flies were going when we got to the river, but no trout were rising. I walked to the river before the rest of the family, and a heron lifted off from Rusty's point. Katy walked up beside me, and I told her that once Junker was crouched on that point, throwing short casts at a big trout eating brown drakes, and nearly got struck by lightning. In my memory it blew his hat off, but I don't trust my memory and neither should anyone that reads this journal. Anyway, Junker never caught the trout. I wouldn't forget that part.

The white flies had started. The white flies are beautiful. They hatch and spin on the same evening without ever touching land. They molt in mid-air and tow their translucent aura-skin with their fairy-tails a few feet above the river before collapsing from their one crazy night.

I went back to the car to rig everyone up. The kids struggled into their waders and played soccer with one of my Crocs and Double-A fell and hurt his knee and I was trying to get everybody rigged up and my back was killing me and finally I yelled, loudly, at both of them.

The game plan: Katy would take the trail downstream and check out a few favorite backwaters down there (as we discussed the plan, a *good* fish rose in the lower backwater). I'd station

Holden in a good, safe spot and let him fish by himself. Double-A and I would fish at the head of the bubble line together.

It's a complex stretch of river. Above us, the river flowed in three channels around two islands. The tail of the first island created a seam where the first and second channels met. The first channel was the size of, say, the mainstream of the Au Sable up by the lodge. The second channel was twice that size. The third channel was obscured behind the second island, which formed the bank of the middle channel. In other words, it's the complicated, niched sort of spot that has a lot going for it. In the old days, us teenagers used to fish downstream by the big clay bank and Rusty and his brother Jim would fish up here. They knew the back way into their spot, while we, full of youthful vigor, forded the main river to get to ours.

A fish rose a few times at the base of Rusty's bubble line, and Holden moved to cast at it.

"Now watch behind you and wait until I'm out of the way."

Hooked me right in the ear!

He was already frustrated from the bass-less day, and I thought maybe this wouldn't work out. Double-A had tangled the fly around his tip-top, and I was distractedly picking at it while watching the river. This is the sort of half-hearted, unfocused crap I do that, by the time I'm dead, will have robbed me of hours of my life. But in this instance—and maybe a handful of others—it allowed me to spot, at a great distance, the rise of a big trout.

The mood shifted in me. I don't know how else to describe it. I just sort of became unmoored.

I grabbed both boys, one in each arm, told them to hang onto their rods, and we forded the first channel so we could fish the middle one where I'd spied the big trout. The river was fast and my back hurt. I set Holden up on the big fish. I plopped him in water up to his belly. There was something not right with my head. None of it felt right, or safe, and something about the night—the white flies, the universal frustration, this one big rising trout—had unmoored me from fatherhood.

"There's the fish," I said briskly when it rose.

I left Holden there and led Double-A upstream for some of the smaller fish that were dotting the surface in a pebbly little run. Chubs maybe. And then Holden got tangled. So I left Double-A there ("Don't move—you can drown in this water") and went back to Holden and untangled the mess for him. The trout was big. It was a big damn trout. It was sliding all over a tail-out, head and tail rising. I think head and tail rises are beautiful. I think white flies are beautiful.

"See the fish?" I said unnecessarily.

"Yes," Holden said, frustrated too.

I went back to Double-A who was standing there in his giant waders admiring the white flies. I heard Holden pull line from his reel and begin to cast, and figured on a tangle. I crouched down next to Double-A, trying to moor myself.

Father. Be a father. *"Okay, buddy, we're going to make some nice casts at these . . ."*

"Got him! Got him GOT HIM GOT HIM!" Holden yelled.

"Stay here," I said to Double-A.

I turned to see Holden, fly-rod up and throbbing, two hands on the cork, spray flying from his reel, line stretched far across the river, sun setting, white fly spinners sweeping across the river in both air and reflection, and Holden unlike I'd ever seen Holden, except for when he pinned a kid in wrestling. It was a match that spring, and he was way behind going into the third, and the other kid was on top, and I was sick of wrestling and sick of high school gyms and sick of winter and sick of . . . and then Holden reversed position and pinned the kid, who I think was stunned and fell into a state of shock. We called it the Immaculate Pin. Holden exploded and put his arms up as if he had just won Junior Nationals.

"I can't believe I got him! I can't believe I got him! I can't believe I got him!" Holden yelled across the river. The water was to the top of his waders and I couldn't believe I'd left him there balanced on the precipice of drowning.

That trout was on the move. That trout had no intention of staying in the middle channel and was sprinting downriver toward where the channels converged. Shit! I ran back and grabbed Double-A, left my rod on the bank, grabbed Holden on the run, told him to keep reeling, and we forded the river to the bank of what is the second island—now across from where we started. The kids shifted in my grip, sideways. Holden recovered line. The current pushed. It was deep. Deep. I leapt to keep them above water. Completely unmoored. Then, safe.

I set Double-A on the bank and told him to wait and grabbed Holden and chucked him over the log that the fish— any sane fish—should have run into and broken us off on. So here we are, I figured, dealing with an insane fish and the sort of persistent back spasm that typically requires cortisone and Oxycontin.

I left Holden fast to his fish, and retrieved Double-A and chucked him, and myself, over the log. Holden regained his fly line and was working it cautiously.

"Don't move!" I yelled at Double-A, pointing at him. He gave me the thumbs up and nodded.

I carried Holden through a deep mucky pool, tripping once and filling my waders but keeping the boy dry.

I ran back and grabbed Double-A and repeated the process. This was serious adventure business. I threw Double-A onto the bank (*Jesus Christ, Dad!*) and ran down to the river, extending the net along the way, dripping sweat and completely unmoored, unmoored from almost everything, including the trout and the kids and Katy. It was cosmic.

I directed Double-A, again, to stay on the bank and I flicked on my light—as it was dark now—and Holden led the fish in. I netted it and fell backward and yelled upward and

Holden was fluttery saying *Holy crap*, and I yelled again. By now Katy had come up to see if we had all drowned, and she was across the river from us watching silently like she does. We did a quick picture. It was a fat, young, big trout. Not a mark on it. It probably weighed three pounds. It didn't swim off. We let it go and it just slid, slowly, beneath the undercut of the bank.

Sometimes I think of all the trout sitting in shallow undercuts and it makes my mind brim pleasantly with possibilities.

Afterward I told Holden that he owed someone a thank-you and he thanked me and I said not me, and so he thanked Double-A. Then I explained that Double-A had given up his whole night because Holden had hooked that fish. And then I told him that Katy and I had talked about hiring a babysitter and going fishing and that *Mom* would have caught that fish.

"Would you have carried her across the river?" Holden said wryly.

Double-A was very excited. He went home and drew a picture of the entire day. And it was very special because of it. I'm drinking beer and mooring, I'm mooring, and trying to get this all down and even as I'm writing I feel the magic escaping from the words like mayflies lifting from a riffle.

September 2

Last night, Katy and I floated the Chute down to the Lab in the canoe. The kids were with the grandparents. Finally, we could go mousing together. It had been a while. It had been fifteen years, we figured, since we'd last gone night fishing together and so we brought a few drinks to celebrate.

Shortly after launching, we saw a red light from a wading angler and navigated around it. "I wade slower than my husband," the red light explained. Then another red light: the husband. By voice, we recognized each other: Todd and Heather, customers of the fly shop. We chatted briefly. Like us, they'd found a sitter for their kids and had chosen to spend their date night on the river. Then, pleasantries exchanged, I moved the canoe downstream.

I paddled down to the bluff overlooking one of my favorite bends in the river, a delicious dark pool filled with logjams and stories. I'd fished the pool since I was a teenager. I decided to walk the canoe through the pool and let Katy fish it methodically. I told her to fish the left side and to lift the rod to accelerate the fly, to wake it across the surface. Then I told her to look up at the hill above the pool, where the big pines stood leaning over the river in the dark. The trees were old white pines. Their roots were in the earth a hundred feet over our head, and their branches were well above that. In the dark, they seemed to climb right into the stars.

I asked her if she was fishing or just casting.

"Just casting, I guess," she said.

And then wham!

It was not a huge brown trout. But it was a brown trout. It ate right in the deepest part of the pool, just on the inside of the bend, and I could feel the happiness in the spine of the canoe as she fought it. She hooked it in deep water and I made a mess of the net job, ultimately doing more splashing and thrashing than the fish. Still, we landed it, skipped the picture, admired the equal red and black spotting on the trout's flanks. We celebrated with a drink: a mix of ginger beer and bourbon and mint she'd made for the float. We drank right from the thermos. It was nice to be pulled over on the sandbar and having a drink with my wife in a pool I'd fished since I was a teenager. I told Katy about the fly shop kids running through the dark woods trying to catch big fish all night from this bend, or how we'd wade down from the bridge pitching prototype hoppers along the grassy banks during hot summer days. The stories revived memories into pleasant ghosts around us, Rusty and Terry and old Tom, all of them, all the history I'd known of the river.

Back at the launch, we ran into Todd and Heather—they, like us, were done fishing for the evening. We stood by the misting river. They were barely older than us. Heather thin and athletic and Todd tall, with a serious face, and a slow, careful demeanor. We stood together talking. Todd and Heather talked about their family, their past. I knew Todd had quit drinking, that his son loved fly-fishing and cooking, that they still followed some of their favorite bands. We talked about bands. They talked about their older daughters, whom I hadn't met, and they talked about the journeys of their daughters, and then the journeys of their own lives, and how hard it is to watch the mistakes of youth, and yet, you know, how fun it was to live those mistakes *as* youth.

I told them about how I met Katy. She'd gone to Ohio University, and the first person she'd met there was one of my best friends growing up. Eventually, that initial meeting, through a few twists and turns, led to us meeting in Oxford three years later. That was nearly twenty years ago—2002. We shared a lot of music then and were a lot younger and full of youthful problems and youthful adventure, and slowly this life together began, accelerating rapidly, producing offspring and accruing age and frustration and wisdom and, at times, perfection.

Our conversation was, or seemed, especially candid on the banks of the misting river, with the cartoonish night flies secured in the hook keepers of our fly rods and the screens of their extinguished headlamps glinting in the starlight, and all of us, you know, kids at heart. There's something to being so alive and twenty-one and hopeful and pumped full of the good juices. And there's something to being forty or more, and standing there at 1:00 a.m. talking about the good old days as if these weren't still them and knowing, of course, that they are.

"I've never seen the northern lights," Heather said. I don't remember how we got to that, but we got to that.

We stared up at the sky and realized that, in fact, she was seeing them, for the first time, right then. They danced faintly above the dark pines. We didn't really speak. Just: There they are. They are lights in the sky. They are electric and luminescent. They are beautiful for no reason.

Which brings forth a different memory:

A decade ago or more, before kids, a friend called me on a dead cold November night and told me to go outside. I went outside. I stared up to the sky. I went inside and woke up Katy.

The sky was on green fire.

We drove to a fishing access known as Guide's Rest and parked on the little hill by the sign. I put our New Zealand sleeping bags—still zipped together—on the pickup bed and we lay there and it was so cold, it was nearly zero, and the lights danced through the sky so bright and subaquatically shimmery it seemed we'd leapt into a bottomless deep pool of river water. The light, or beauty, or both, had an unmanageable intensity. It pinched a nerve in me. The auroras flowered in spectacular pulses, each brighter than the last. When we left, it was out of exhaustion from the massiveness of it. Try thinking about infinity for two hours and that is how I felt. A human can only take so much cosmic power.

September 3

Today I snatch Double-A from home and we put the long-boat in the water at Thendara. It's mid-afternoon, highs in the low 70s. Holden's white fly fish has inspired Double-A to go fly-fishing. He's been tying inventive and terrible flies on giant, expensive hooks. He wants to fish his flies. His flies are four inches long, weigh an ounce, and often have other hooks lashed onto the shank—a homemade treble hook of sorts. I have to make a deal involving a candy bar for him to fish one of mine: A size 14 cinnamon flying ant. On a September afternoon, the cinnamon ant should be the ticket.

We get to the river and I give him the rundown and leave him be, and he starts casting and the boy is INTO it. Watching his fly. Spotting risers. It does not take long and he has his first solo trout on the fly . . . a brook trout. As is his nature, his hat is sideways just so, reflective shades, and a confident smirk. It's easy, he declares. So easy.

On the ride to the river he'd told me he wanted a rainbow, and his second trout is just that. It ate when we weren't watching, and is hooked when Double-A starts his back cast, and then he, in Double-A fashion, explains that he saw it all happen. Saw the rainbow eat the fly. It's complete fabrication. But he repeats it, embellishing: he'll will me to see it as his imagination sees it. And I do see it. I do.

After that, the boy puts down the rod. He puts his knees on the floor of the boat, and puts his head an inch from the water, and commands me to paddle. I oblige. *Faster.* I oblige. *Much faster.* I give it all I got. The trout in the clear September water scatter from the blade shadow of the riverboat. They bury into the weeds until there are too many, and scatter again, joining and rejoining, merging seamlessly back into invisibility.

Just above the take-out, an osprey explodes the water behind us and climbs slowly, skims my head. I could have hit it with my boat pole. By the time it passes Double-A, it's ten feet and climbing. We watch it go, talons empty. It missed the fish, I explain.

"I'm better at fishing than that bird," Double-A says. He turns in the boat and flashes his shit-eating grin back at me. "Way better."

CHAPTER 7: GONE DOG

"After the initial mistake, the errors tend to compound."

—Attributed to Ernest Hemingway, from the
book *Papa Hemingway* by A. E. Hotchner

November 14 – November 16

About thirty hours ago, I took my friends from Ohio, Matt and Dan Bartow, to my best grouse spot.

It's a spot I discovered while guiding the river for trout. It was a fall float then, in the mid-2000s, and we were near the end of our float when I saw a Brittany spaniel on point in an alder thicket. The dog had a bell but the bell was, and had been, silent. This was a long-standing point. The dog knew we were there but didn't break its concentration on the unseen bird. Not when we were fifty feet away. Not even as we floated ten feet by. Far in the distance I could hear the dog's owners calling for their dog. That dog wasn't doing anything but standing at bird scent. I floated by silently. Never said a word to my clients. Never heard a shot. Never heard a bell.

I didn't have a bird dog then. But I knew right away I wanted one.

I didn't have a spot to take a bird dog either. I knew I wanted one of those too.

Once I got a couple of bird dogs I decided to find the easy way back to that spot—one that didn't require me to cross the river. This was before Google Maps and other, even more useful smartphone apps. Then, it was harder and more fun to ferret out access to such spots (but, in case you're wondering, I *do* use those apps, because grouse season is short and my shooting is bad). I bumped around in the general direction of a spot until I found it. Scouting missions were conducted with little regard to time or success. When I found *this* spot, it was with sixth sense. It just seemed that the little two-track that hooked around a big oak tree had to be it. I couldn't tell just by the parking spot. I had to walk around, walk down, until I came to the river. Once I was on the river, then I knew.

The covert, like a good trout run, had multiple components: a jack pine thicket, an oak flat, several poplar thickets, several grassy fields, a stand or two of red pine, whole clumps of thorn apple trees, one long cedar swamp, a thin line of alders, and then the river.

I hunted this spot for years, and I learned how it hunts differently in different months, the way it changes and seems to age and mature until, late in the first grouse season (which runs from September 15 through November 14), it has ripened into a grouse spot so fecund with grouse and promise that, in the lexicon of trout holes, it resembles none other than that swirly Henry's Fork flat on a warm night in May. The name I gave the spot reveals its location. So instead, here's another name: Gone Dog.

 ⌒

Matt Bartow and I grew up together in Ohio. We set up adventure mountain bike races in our backyards, we played endless hours of basketball, we struggled through AP English, and I even taught him to fly-fish. In high school, he aced the math section of one of those military prep tests, aced college, and ended up being an ace at Boeing out in Seattle. His dad, Dan, was always my baseball coach. A plumber, Dan maintained his sprawling farm not for crops but for wild quail, which he didn't shoot but instead saved to train his own line of German shorthairs. I wasn't a hunter until my mid-twenties. But once I was, Dan Bartow—once a friend's father—became a friend himself. He instructed me on bird hunting by lending books, campfire advice, and showing me, through his shorthairs, how a hunting dog is meant to be.

This past fall, Matt emailed me that he was planning a grouse trip to Michigan with his dad. It was to be the last two days of the first bird season, November 13 and 14. On November 15, the grouse woods became deer woods, and the grouse season was closed until December. The dates of their visit were prime time to visit Gone Dog, which, that fall, had been exceptionally good to me . . . better, in truth, than any grouse spot I'd ever hunted. I was somewhat eager to share it with someone, especially people who lived no less than seven hours from it. I think we share secret spots to share ourselves. I've only kept a few spots from everyone. There is a trout seam I've never shared with anyone. It's just one seam. But I'll share it one day because a trout seam is a fragile thing and I don't want the seam to disappear before I can show it to someone. I've lost trout spots to the gentle shift of the factors that created them. A stick moves, the river bottom changes, and suddenly the magic is gone. Such spots come and go like miracles, and sometimes you lament not sharing them.

In preparation for Matt and Dan's visit, I had elk steaks from a friend, and grouse breasts that would be dusted in ground-up wild rice and fried in bacon fat and served with cranberry sauce over wild rice, wood duck, goose strips, great bourbon, greater scotch, two fit dogs, excellent coffee, and a vehicle that still operated.

Matt and his father arrived in a snowstorm and stayed at the lodge. They were the only ones there. That first night, we drank about a hundred beers by the fireplace in the suite, petted Dan's dogs Jack and Molly, and debated marijuana legalization. At about midnight, while staring out the window, I decided that I could watch November snowflakes fly past patio lights for the rest of my life. The rush of the season wasn't merely over; winter was here.

To a deer hunter excited for the opening day of rifle season in the north woods, a snowy forecast allows easy tracking, and it's easier to see the brown deer slinking through the forest. To the grouse hunter, however, snow is an adversary: snow dumping off pine boughs and down the back of hunting coats, grouse flushing from trees, ice accumulating into painful ice balls between the toes of the hard-working dogs.

It snowed sideways on the drive to Gone Dog. It was a greasy November snow, the kind that slides under the wipers and smears the windshield with a blinding white patina. The Bartows—father and son—are both tall, strong, optimistic people that value hard work and hard conditions. I've never really heard them lament a situation beyond their control. Matt and I really did play a lot of basketball together and would find pickup games on the outdoor courts around

Oxford. He had a tiny little white car, an ancient old car, and it could hold about two dollars worth of gas because of a hole in the fuel tank. We'd fill up at the farm, drive into town, play a ton of basketball, lap at nearby water fountains, go back to the gas station, pay with more change (we're talking like 87 cents of gas), and putter on home.

Which is to say, the Bartows were unfazed by the snow. It was a condition that would add to future stories told around future fireplaces as future snow fell past future patio lights.

We parked the trucks on the upper plateau, and began by heading north up the ridge toward a stand of pines. The grouse, driven to roost in the pines by the snow, flushed wildly from the treetops: twenty, thirty, forty feet above the dogs. They were everywhere. More, it seemed, than I'd ever seen before. Dan, who counts flushes, said we were at seventeen birds, and we were not even a half-hour in. The birds were flushing from trees or dense thickets of jack pine, the flush revealed by the thunder in their wings and the briefest glimpse of mottled feather. We had almost zero clear shots at a bird. Jack, the older male dog, nailed a nice point, and Molly, the young up-and-comer, honored. It was a running bird that blew up beyond a clump of jack pine. It was snowing sideways, and windy. A minute later, I took a shot at a bird that flushed from the top of a red pine, just because. Matt did too, and explained it was "to keep the barrel warm."

"I've never seen this many grouse in one place," Dan said.

I was glowing.

"Hang on," Dan said. "Where's Jack?"

We called his name. No big deal. The hunt had only begun and there were grouse everywhere in these woods and the dog, I knew, couldn't be far. We hollered and blew the whistle but our noise seemed to be absorbed by the snow. We fanned out but I wasn't yet worried. The dog had been right next to us. He'd be here any second, bell jingling, ready to find more grouse.

Now, I've had dogs go missing. Most hunters have. And here's how it usually goes: for about fifteen minutes, we blow whistles and we fret and we pace and we're *just* about to call someone, and then the dog returns. But Jack stayed missing.

We spread out farther through the woods. Grouse flushed in twos and threes and more. They busted from beneath snow-covered spruces, from a cluster of jack pines, from a deadfall beneath an oak. We'd quit hunting and were now just looking for the missing dog, but it was clear what sort of hunting day we'd have had on that windy, snowy, November day if Jack hadn't gone missing. We circled and looked, reconvened, discussed possible fates for Jack. The most likely was a porcupine.

We searched the rest of the day. We followed tracks we thought were his tracks. We followed tracks that turned out to be Molly's tracks. We backtracked our tracks. We sweated and cursed and called. One tree—I swear, one tree—had a dozen or more grouse flush from it. Yes, it was the day that I'd meant us to have. We all grimly knew it. It just wasn't the day we were having.

When the day faded behind the western hill, we set Dan's old sweaters in the snow in case the dog came back, and we backtracked our hunting route endlessly, until our socks were soup, until our paths in the snow—now moonlit—crossed into helixes that laced across my coveted covert. By 10:00 p.m.— four hours after dark—we sadly figured that he had tangled with a porcupine, that he'd been quilled to the point of incapacitation, and that we wouldn't find him in the dark.

But you can't just quit.

So we began driving around and blowing the whistle. I drove every logging road I knew. I imagined that dog could hear us—hear everything, like dogs can—and couldn't respond. That, if we were lucky, we would find him a few dozen yards from our boot tracks, jaws locked around a porcupine, hundreds of quills projecting like guard hairs across his head. I imagined him there under that silver moon shivering beneath a spruce, voice hoarse, beeper battery long since dead, and not a howl in his throat to save him.

We ate the saddest, best dinner I could muster. It was terrible.

The next morning we began searching deadfalls, looking now for a frozen bird dog. We spread out and worked in a grid, the inaccuracies in our straight lines recorded in the snow. I spoke to the folks who owned the big tract of land to the north, who were preparing their deer camp, who politely told me that I wasn't allowed on their property, missing dog or not. We put more tracks on the public land; our footprints in the fresh snow overlapping the rounded ones we'd left the day before.

By 3:00 p.m. I was spent, and headed home for a nap, then to prepare my deer hunting gear and my component of deer camp dinner. But the missing dog was now on social media, thanks to Katy, and as I lay down I realized I'd missed a call from my friend Duane, who said that he'd read on Facebook that a shorthair was running down Chase Bridge Road, by Forest Dunes, wearing an orange collar. This sighting was some fifteen miles from where we'd been hunting, and twenty-four hours after the dog had gone missing. I grabbed a coffee and hit the road, pushing every mph of the new M-72 speed limit.

I called Matt, who was still at the old hunting spot kicking deadfalls, and told him that I was en route to a possible sighting. "But there are a lot of shorthairs in this county," I said.

I flew down Chase Bridge Road, a cloud of snow behind me. I drove past Forest Dunes, and past Thayer Creek, and turned around at 7-Mile.

As I headed north, on the right side of the road, like a winter's mirage, stood Jack. Collar on. Bell dangling. And his telltale marking: a left front leg sleeved in brown fur. There was slobber frozen to his face and his eyes were feral, wild, sparkling.

Giddy—I'd been imagining this dog for hours, had seen him even in dreams the night before—I slammed on the brakes, and, ready to deliver this dog finally back to his home, I exited and yelled his name, and his command—"Jack come!"

The dog, scared and cold and wanting only his true owner, fled. He fled up into the hills.

And though I was soon joined by Matt and Dan, and though we searched and blew the whistle and called *JACK!* to the stars, and though the coyotes wailed and the deer hunters paused from their deer camps to listen with us, we could not hear an answering bark or whimper, or even the jingling of the bell.

No fancy dinners that night. We had a drink, and I bid my old buddy Matt Bartow goodbye—he had to go back to his family in Seattle. Dan planned on staying. Well, he threatened to leave, figuring the dog was a goner, but we knew he'd stay. I went to the Verlac's house—along with Katy and the kids—for very strong Manhattans and a sense of normalcy. It was deer camp after all: the magical night before the opening morning of the deer rifle-hunting season. Verlac would be hunting the next morning. I, exhausted, would not. I told the story as I've told it here, sipping Katrina's deadly Manhattans laced with Katy's homemade maraschino cherries. Their pack of dogs entertained the children. The fireplace churned heat and flame. Reggae on the radio, snow in the porch light. There is so much movement right before the winter buries it all.

The next morning was the opening day of rifle season in Michigan. I skipped it and began driving. Occasionally, I'd pass Dan's vehicle, also on the search. It was 7 degrees. About 10:00 a.m. I abandoned the search and took the kids to the local buck pole—a pole on which the big bucks shot on Opening Morning were hung for admiration—so they could see the big, dead deer their dad always fails to shoot. On the way back home, my phone rang. It was a friend reporting that *the* dog was in his yard on Wakeley Bridge Road. Coincidentally, this friend lives in our old house. The dog was (kind of) in my yard! Now ten miles north of where I'd seen him the day before.

I told the kids we were en route to a rescue and I floored it down North Down, and hung a right on Wakeley. I excitedly called Dan and told him to get his ass to Wakeley Bridge. Near the Lower Trout Unlimited property I saw the Crawford County Animal Control truck headed the opposite direction. I flagged her down and she reported that she'd seen the dog, had tried to catch him, and the dog had fled into the woods. I sped down the road toward where she'd seen the dog, and I saw Dan's vehicle headed my way.

He was the very next vehicle.

We were one minute from rescue. If Animal Control hadn't been there, it would have been Dan that saw Jack, it would have been Dan's whistle, Dan's voice, and finally, after over forty-eight hours, Dan's dog once again.

Still, we tried, standing there on Wakeley Bridge Road.

Dan blew the whistle toward the forest. The kids and I blocked Wakeley Bridge, figuring the dog would take the bridge instead of the icy river. We listened for the bell. The dog was gone. It was heartbreaking.

That afternoon I deer-hunted while Dan drove the county. I let a small buck walk past me only to hear him get shot farther down the ridge. I left the stand after that.

Dan called to tell me that he'd driven through several tanks of gas, but the dog remained gone. Meanwhile, there were little pings here and there, deer hunters who'd heard the ghostly sound of a bell in the forest at first light, at last light. A ghost, by now, a dog met only in dream. We knew he was alive. We also knew that he wasn't anyone's fool. This was

Dan's dog to find, and no one else would do. And I think, if Dan had left, Jack the dog would have kept running across the county until he collapsed.

The next morning, on a hunch, Dan returned to where we'd lost the dog originally, at my secret grouse spot. A deer hunter's black jeep was parked there.

Dan got out of his vehicle, and cleared his throat in preparation to call, for the thousandth time, *Jack!* when from under the black jeep slunk a shivering, skinny, exhausted dog, telltale leg sleeved in brown, ribs bending his skin.

Jack, who had spent three nights and a round trip thirty miles in sub-freezing temperatures, undoubtedly crashing through ice, crossing midnight bridges, feasting, when he could, on deer gut piles, all the while searching for one person on Earth while several people on Earth searched for him.

Dan and I spoke before he left for Ohio. He was pulling out of the lodge and he lowered the window of his truck. "Well," he said. "He's pretty whipped. I thought about leaving, but Sue called me and told me to just go back to where we started because she figured he was looking for me. And now I guess she was right. I figure he was just going through everywhere he thought I'd been," he said.

"I'll bet he came down through the campground where I stayed earlier this fall, and I guess he probably made his way to the Chapel cause that's where he pointed that double, and when you saw him he was looping around to that spot you showed me, and from there, I guess, he was gonna loop back up and keep looking."

As he spoke, Jack crawled up between the two front seats and licked Dan's face. Both looked equally exhausted in my estimation. It was a county-wide love story measured in gallons of gas.

I left the lodge that afternoon and I went directly to bed. I slept almost impossibly well, too deeply to call it a nap. I woke and it was dark. There was a moment of panic. I stayed prone, and forced the panic away. The dog was found. The grouse season was over. It was just an event that had to be dealt with. It seemed a pretty big thing at the time. The biggest. The outdoors can propel me toward a small point of concentration so bright and hot I see its afterimage flashing between me and my normal life, like a river beside a mountain road. I can't keep my eyes off it, no matter how sharp the turns.

⌇

When you go in pursuit of trout you will inevitably meet kindred spirits, and your fascination with fly-fishing will bind you in a pure way. The joy of this is eventually balanced by the sadness of losing the people to whom you've been bound so purely. I see the way winter has worn people when they walk into the shop in the spring, the shadow of their skin-walker growing longer across their faces. Within minutes, then, the promise of trout water invades, resurrects, and they draw the power to wade into the ever-increasing flows of the gentle Au Sable. One year, they too must sit on the bench and marvel at the speed of the water and the dance of the small trout in the bubble lines and the brilliance of this thing that, like the northern lights, is beautiful for no reason at all.

Perhaps I'll get to that, too. I hope so. That would be a good spot to be, just remembering all the adventures, and grooving on things being beautiful for no reason at all.

Several years ago, in the dead of winter, in what we will all think of as the good old days as this journal is being revised and published during the 2020 pandemic shutdown, I decided to make the most of a good winter forecast and go full-hooky and spend a whole day fishing. In fact, I craved a doubleheader of trout fishing. First, ice fishing with my friend and river guide Jordan, and then river fishing with Verlac. As I said, this was several years ago, and my kids at the time were much younger. Double-A was not even in preschool, and Holden was halfway through kindergarten. It was winter and the shop was slow, and Aaron would be at daycare and Holden in school.

There was a science fair at Holden's school that night and the whole family would go. I promised to attend, though I did so without considering whether it was logistically possible for me to complete the entire, two-part day of fishing and still make it to the science fair. Still, the boy said there'd be animals, including raptors, and that didn't sound all that bad.

The First Act began with an hour-long drive to a secret trout lake that I can never seem to remember how to get to on the first try. My fishing companion Jordan is something of a fishing nut. He's a fly-fishing guide, sure, but Jordan just likes to fish with the same tinkering obsessiveness you might see at a robotics convention, or a Rubik's Cube competition. When he's not guiding he's fishing, and when he's not fishing he's tying flies. Jordan and I jigged up a few trout from the ice hole, and laughed at the ones we lost. We had the lake to ourselves that morning, but the surface was riddled with old holes, a few of which hadn't frozen over. Some corn was sprinkled around one of these un-frozen holes, and trout being suckers for corn, we figured the angler who'd drilled the hole had either been using the corn as bait or was using it as chum. That wasn't the weird part. The weird part was what looked to be a discarded, frozen, slightly undersized trout next to the still unfrozen ice hole. Closer inspection revealed it to be a pretty massive mudpuppy. Had this guy caught it and chucked it on the ice to suffocate and freeze? Or did the mudpuppy swim up from the bottom, climb through the hole, and freeze to death while eating the corn? Who knows? But I pocketed the frozen mudpuppy to show the kids, in the name of science.

I have reason to believe that, over three years later, it's still in my freezer.

After Jordan and I were done fishing, and without changing from my ice fishing bibs, Verlac and I began the Second Act by loading up the raft and fishing stuff and deciding, against all good advice and experience, to drive into the Mason Tract, drop the raft halfway between the bridges, and spot the truck down at Smith Bridge. The roads inside the Tract were pretty good owing to a winter's worth of logging. Logging doesn't seem as bad for our rivers as western rivers—we are geographically too flat for rampant erosion and run-off—but when the logging is done in the middle of winter, it still seems like a secret hit job on the forests.

Way back in the winter wilds, it's very much a life-and-death game. We found a deer that had been torn to shreds by some coyotes. It was pretty fresh and pretty gruesome, and all that was left was the stomach and fur. It was probably late at night. Maybe a little moon: the sounds of joy and terror. The killing had happened along the road. This was no desecrated road kill. An animal had been pack-hunted and torn apart, spilling steam and blood across the winter.

The river was beautiful. All the rivers are beautiful in the winter, but the South Branch is just so wild . . . when you're halfway through the float, in a big still stretch that the guides paddle through in the summer, you're about as far from hardtop as you can get in Crawford County. The land around it is dotted with beaver ponds that are connected by a series of feeder creeks. It is tough walking through the woods. The trout are as tough and wild as the river valley is.

Along the way we found somebody's old hut or teepee or whatever it was—a pretty tidy cone of logs, reflective thermal blankets, a blue tarp, and a bunch of paracord. The inside was a bed of spruce branches. There was an old creamer packet in there from the morning coffee. There were no tracks in the snow, so we tore it down, removing the plastics and the ropes.

The water was low and pretty clear, which I think are the best conditions when the water temperatures are cold. It makes sense, really. What fish wants to fight high, cold water? We started out with the same fly we realized we'd been fishing all winter: an off-yellow streamer we call a Wedge-head. In fact, it was the only fly we'd used all winter, at least on our floats together. Not just a style of fly, but *the* very fly. Tied on *the* leader. Attached to *the* rod. And since December, the fly and leader we'd fished every Tuesday. The fly had held form pretty well, but the paint had long since worn off the weighted eyes, and the marabou had thinned, and the hooks probably needed a good sharpening. But it was the tippet that failed us.

That tippet had been tugged, twisted, spun, and retrieved from any number of tangles and clusters, and proved no match for a hard-charging trout that clean broke me off and then sat there on the bottom trying to shake *the* fly from its mouth . . .

which it did. The fly rested on the black muck of the bottom, with three feet of very cold water separating us.

"We had that coming," I said. "That's just bad fishing."

"Want to get the fly?" Verlac said.

I looked at the water. The water looked very cold. "Not particularly."

We tied on the same fly in black, which was probably the right fly to begin with. The trout were on the hunt. That's how it is in the winter. One minute the fishing sucks. The next minute, the trout are on the hunt. In the next hundred yards of river, I lost another trout right at the net that was nearly as big as the one I broke off, and then I caught a giant male brown with a huge hooked jaw that shot from a logjam like a spear, and I thought for sure was a pike. He fought *hard*, and kept his hook-jaw pointing downward under the boat as we rowed to the bank and swooped the net beneath it. The trout looked big in the net. It was an old trout, pocked by the years, and nearly two feet long. There are some trout that are young and big and fresh, and one year from the South—also with Verlac—I'd landed such a trout: a green-backed fish that was probably five pounds that ate an upstream cast foam fly on a full moon, and was the prettiest trout my flashlight has ever illuminated. This winter trout wasn't that. But it was definitely the trout of the day.

After the big trout, it began raining. Matt moved a few more trout and landed one, and then we began to push-row to get off the river. The timing would be tight, I thought, but I should have enough time for a shower and a change of clothes before hightailing it to the science fair, as long as things went well. But of course they didn't go well, or else there'd be no memory of this day. After we'd pulled the raft up onto the bank at the landing, I realized I'd left the tie-downs in my truck. With no way to secure the raft, we headed back to get my tie-downs and my truck. But the snowy Mason Tract roads were a problem . . . the rain had made them soft. Even Verlac's quasi-monster truck struggled. We decided it would be faster to get my truck and take the road out to Chase Bridge—the nearest hard top—and then drive all the way back around to Smith Bridge. Instead of a fifteen-minute car spot, it took about an hour. And during that time it rained and iced constantly, and that rain must have accumulated in the raft and pooled up in the stern. This extra weight would be the best theory as to why the raft slid down the snowy ramp and into the river and floated, unmanned, downstream while we were miles away trying not to slide into the ditch.

When we finally made it back to the boat launch, the raft was long gone. We sprinted along the river, through the dark, icy woods without flashlights, plunging into sticks and deadfalls. My ice fishing bibs—which I'd worn all day—were soaked. I felt like I was wearing a huge sponge of cold water. The woods were a slushy, snowy mess, my glasses were so fogged I couldn't have seen the raft anyway. Verlac finally spotted the craft lodged into a logjam across the river from us. It had drifted a half-mile downstream. Phew. Verlac crossed the river without waders to get the raft, and we tied it to a tree for removal the following day and then sprinted through the dripping woods. Late, late for the science fair!

The drive was through that same kind of greasy, slick snow as that day on the way to Gone Dog. And perhaps that what triggered this memory. Or perhaps it was the gone raft, and the odd way we pursue things that are lost as if we must be the ones that are found. No matter, my memory is so inconsistent I guess I'm just glad when an unexpected remembrance arrives, no matter the lineage. I've never kept a really detailed journal, and I'm not nearly analytical enough to record trout-y things like water temperatures and barometric pressures and river levels. People like me aren't fishing for the trout. We're just fishing. It's a direction, not a location. When a dog goes missing, you know exactly what you're looking for. But when in trout water, I'm not looking for trout so much as the state of being that the pursuit of trout gives me.

I made it to the science fair at the last possible minute. Holden was inside a closed classroom staring—along with a bunch of other kids—at a man with an owl on his forearm. I barged through the door, sopping wet, sticks in my hair, and nearly ran over the teacher stationed there to prevent interruption, and sat next to my kindergartner, who paused from his earnest study of the owl to stare at me. His class, the man with the owl on his arm, and even the owl stared at me. They had all the wonder in the world, and so did I. Holden tugged on the soggy elbow of my wool sweater and stared at me darkly, his face serious.

"Hi Dad," he whispered. "Did you catch a big one?"